Ten By Ten: Book Four

Ten 10-Minute Plays

Kenneth P. Langer

Brass Bell Books

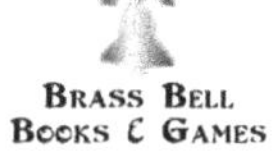

10 X 10 Book Four
A Collection of Ten Ten-Minute Plays
By Kenneth P. Langer

First Edition Version 1.1, 2024

published by Brass Bell Books
www.brassbellbooks.com

The author may be contacted at klangerdude@gmail.com

Contents

Introduction

READER: Soooo! Book Four of Ten-Minute Plays, huh? Bet you never thought you would get so far along.

AUTHOR: I was fairly certain that Book Three would be the last in the collection.

READER: Why?

AUTHOR: Well, so many book series come in trilogies. Besides, my life literally fell apart after I wrote nine of the ten plays in Book Three. It took quite a bit of determination to finish the last play. It would be three years before I could find the strength to tackle another one.

READER: Oh? Terrible tragedy, you say? Sounds like a lot of pain and suffering, angst and anger, sturm und drang, fits of wailing through the night... Want to talk about it?

AUTHOR: No.

READER: You know what they say, don't you? It helps to talk about it.

AUTHOR: You seem a little too anxious to hear about the anguish and not about the strong feelings involved.

READER: Anger, yelling, scream, misery! All good stuff.

AUTHOR: It's rather personal, you know. I don't really want to drag up old...

READER: Conflict! Isn't that what makes a great play: the introduction and resolution of conflict? The hero's story is all about overcoming the terrible odds and making it through to the other side. Everybody loves a good hero's story. It can inspire others to weather their own storms. Wouldn't you agree?

AUTHOR: Well, yes but...

READER: Want to talk about it?

AUTHOR: No.

READER: But this is your chance. As a writer you can tell the world your story. You can have the ears of the world. You can capture the hearts of your fans.

AUTHOR: All three of them?

READER: So, what do you say? Want to talk about it?

AUTHOR: No. Suffice it to say that writing these plays was a way to crawl out of the darkness and move forward.

READER: Into the light. Into a new dawn. Forward through the storm like the brave captain...

AUTHOR: I'm not going to talk about it, so drop it!

READER: So Book Four was therapy?

AUTHOR: No. It was post therapy, a celebration of a new era.

READER: And the plays reflect that?

AUTHOR: I certainly hope not. They are meant to be in the same general vein of works as those in the first three books of plays.

READER: But there is one significant difference isn't there?

AUTHOR: What do you mean?

READER: Well, you were ordained as a Universalist minister between Book Three and Book Four.

AUTHOR: Yes. That is true.

READER: And would not that experience affect your writing?

AUTHOR: No more or less than it has before. I am still the same writer with the same convictions. I try to put some small contemplation about life in every play.

READER: Well, your agent made me promise I would mention that little piece of information.

AUTHOR: I don't have an agent.

READER: Must have been your PR person.

AUTHOR: Don't have one.

READER: Publisher?

AUTHOR: No.

READER: Personal assistant? Dog walker? Delivery driver?

AUTHOR: Nope.

READER: Sounds terrible... Want to talk about it?

Synopses

Bench Press

A person sitting on a park bench gets strange prophetic messages from the people passing by.

From The House

A highly improvised, participatory play about three theater goers find out that they are the ones on stage.

Grandma's House

Several fairy tales get mixed up together when their characters come to visit Grandma.

Left Behind

A new employee discovers that being left handed may be an unexpected problem.

Lost In Translation

A job seeker hires a translator who only manages to make matters worse.

October Seventh

At the end of 2012, the leader of a group naming itself the eBible Fellowship predicted that the end of the world would come on October 7, 2015. This play takes place on the day after the end of the world.

Pain In The Neck

A Vampire and a Vampire Hunter meet at a costume party.

Perfect Partner

Two people marry their favorite person then decide to have an affair together.

Tooth Fairy

A single father tries to get a date with the Tooth Fairy.

Too Much Sheet

A customer at a linens store attempts to buy a white sheet but for a mysterious purpose.

Bench Press

A Ten-Minute Comedy

Cast

ALEX - An average sort of person.

PEOPLE (P1-P16) - People who pass from one side of the stage to the other. Different people can be used or a few people can be recycled through by changing costumes and mannerisms.

YOUNG PERSONs (YP1 and YP2) - children

MUSICIAN - a street musician preferably with an instrument like a guitar, drum, or violin

PARENT and CHILD - an adult and a child

WORKER - someone dressed in work clothes carrying a large board.

MUGGER - a grungy looking person with a knife.

THE DOG - If possible, a real dog.

Note1: The parts can be played by persons of any gender or ethnicity. Pronouns may be changed as needed.

Note2: The people passing by should act as if they are in the middle of a conversation. In their lines, the written text is what needs to be clearly heard while all the rest can be unclear and improvised.

Scene

A park. There are two benches near each other facing the audience. There is some random trash under the benches. There is the sound of a dog that is heard intermittently throughout the play. It should start soft and distant and eventually become more obvious.

Time

Present.

Script

[At rise, ALEX is sitting on one bench reading a book or something similar. After a few moments, the first People pass by in front of ALEX but do not pay him any attention.]

P1 and P2: ...this may be your lucky day...

P3, P4: ...are you listening?...

P5, P6: ...a very lucky day...

[ALEX puts down the book and looks in the direction of the people passing by then picks up the book again.]

P7: (*approaches ALEX*) Excuse me! I was wondering if you knew where the money is.

ALEX: The money?

P7: What?

ALEX: You asked where the money was.

P7: Yeah. Demonte. Do you know where Demonte Street is?

ALEX: Oh, Demonte. You said Demonte.

P7: That's right. The money.

ALEX: The money?

P7: That's what I said, Demonte!

ALEX: Uh, Demonte street is three blocks that way. (*points*)

P7: Ah! Thanks. (*starts to walk away*) I hope you find what you're looking for.

ALEX: What I'm looking for? I'm not... Ugh! (*goes back to book*)

[P8 and P9 walk by]

P8: ... I think they're going to go under...

P9: ...are they really going under?..

P8: ...I know, I know I don't UNDERstand...

[ALEX looks curiously at the two people as they pass by then returns to the book. After a few moments a young person runs in front of ALEX as if to catch a ball. The person might have a baseball mitt or a field hockey stick or just their hands up.]

YP: (*with hands in the air*) Here! Here! Right here!

[A ball comes to YP who catches it.]

ALEX: Good catch!

YP: A little close by, huh?

ALEX: What?

YP: It's a good thing I caught it because it came close by!

ALEX: Yeah, thanks.

YP: (*to offstage friend*) I'm coming!

[YP exits and ALEX returns to the book but after a moment he slowly lowers the book and has a look of deep

thought.]

ALEX: Are you listening? Are you listening? Is this a message? (*thinks*) The money? What money? Is there money involved? Am I being sent a message? (*thinks*) Going under? Understand? (*thinks*) Right here? Close by? (*thinks*) Money... Under... Here? Under here? Here?

[ALEX searches under the bench for a few moments then finds a small wad of money.]

ALEX: What's this? A wad of twenty dollar bills? There must be 100 dollars here. Oh my! This IS my lucky day. Wait! It's a lucky DAY not just a lucky moment. There might be more!

[ALEX sits back down on the bench and pretends to read his book but is more interested in who might show up.]

P9, P10 ...someone could get hurt...

P11 (*muttering repeatedly*) We live in dangerous times, dangerous times!

[P11 bumps into ALEX and then moves on]

ALEX: Dangerous times? What dangerous times? I need to know more!

[ALEX runs nervously back and forth looking for more people to come by but none do.]

ALEX: Alright. I just have to be patient and keep my ears open.

[MUSICIAN comes on stage, sits on the other bench, puts out a hat or box for money, and begins to play music. After a moment...]

ALEX: (*to MUSICIAN*) Hey! What are you doing?

MUSICIAN: Playing my music. What do you think I'm doing?

ALEX: You can't be here. I can't hear what people are saying.

MUSICIAN: I can be here just as well as you. If you don't like the music then just move on.

ALEX: Hey look! (*reaches into pocket*) I'll give you twenty dollars if you move to another set of benches.

MUSICIAN: Make it forty and you got a deal.

ALEX: Fine. Forty dollars.

[ALEX takes the money out of his pocket and gives it to the MUSICIAN. PARENT and CHILD cross upstage and then stare toward the back of the stage. ALEX quickly runs back to the bench and pretends to read his book. WORKER comes across the stage carrying a large board.]

CHILD: Look! Look! There's ducks. There's ducks, mommy/daddy. So many ducks!

ALEX: Ducks? Ducks? DUCK!

[As ALEX is saying the last DUCK, the WORKER acts as if looking for something then turns around with the board. ALEX ducks down just in time to miss being hit by the board. WORKER exits.]

PARENT: (*to CHILD*) C'mon. It's time we got back.

[PARENT and CHILD exit.]

ALEX: Whoa! That was close. This really IS a lucky day. I wonder what might happen next.

[ALEX looks to both sides but sees no one. He picks up his book again but keeps looking for more people to come by. After a time, P12 and P13 walk by. They are clearly in love and look longingly at each other but say nothing. They walk slowly and stop for a few moments to enjoy the scene then move slowly to exit. Eventually, ALEX comes

up behind them and follows them until they exit.]

ALEX: (*to the side*) Nothing? You got nothing to say? Nothing at all? (*pause*) You'll break each other's hearts within a year. Take it from me.

[P14 walks by while talking on a cellphone]

P14: (*to phone*) What?.. Yeah... It will happen soon... real soon... (*exits*)

ALEX: What? Something will happen soon? What is it? What?

[ALEX hears sobbing offstage. It is quiet then becomes louder. P15 enters and runs to a bench still crying. ALEX walks to P15.]

ALEX: (*to P15*) What is it? What's wrong?

P15: S/he was the love of my life! Oh...

ALEX: What happened?

[*P15 tries to stop crying and then turns to ALEX. P15 looks at ALEX for a moment as if to speak but then suddenly bursts into tears. P15 runs offstage still crying.*]

ALEX: What did I do? (*sits*) Happen soon... The love of my life... What does it mean? The love of my life will happen soon? (*gasps*) Could it be? Could it really be?

[ALEX paces nervously around the stage muttering to himself and looks anxiously from side to side.]

ALEX: Oh, I have to relax. (*sits*) Just relax and be patient. That's what I need to do. Be patient.

[MUGGER runs on stage, looks around, sees ALEX and runs toward him.]

ALEX: (*to MUGGER*) You? You can't be the one!

MUGGER: I am the one! (*pulls out knife*) I am the one who's going to rob you.

ALEX: Rob me? No! That's not right. I'm supposed to meet the love of my life.

MUGGER: You're gonna meet your maker if you don't give me your wallet right now!

ALEX: But they said I would meet my love.

MUGGER: What are you, some kind of nut? (*to audience*) Why can't I just, for once, find some normal victim, huh? (*to ALEX*) OK, pal. You can listen to all the crazy voices you want once you give me your money.

ALEX: (*thinking*) No, no. This isn't right. Something's not right.

MUGGER: What's not right is you! Now, I'm not going to ask you again. Hand over your cash right now or I'll start putting holes in you.

ALEX: This is not part of the narrative.

MUGGER: (*getting nervous*) Look! I mean it. It's your money or your life!

ALEX: No!

MUGGER: What?

ALEX: I said no. You're in the wrong place or I'm the wrong victim or... I don't know but this isn't supposed to happen and I'm not going to die on this day so... no!

MUGGER: (*more nervous*) I'll kill you. I swear I'll kill you.

ALEX: Go on, then. Stab me.

MUGGER: All right. I'll do it. I'm gonna do it. Here I go. You're gonna be sorry.

ALEX: Come on then.

[ALEX and MUGGER stare at each other until MUGGER gets frustrated and runs off stage leaving the knife on the bench. ALEX picks up the knife. There is a sound offstage as P16 enters looking dirty and unkept. P16 may be carrying items or pushing a cart. ALEX hides the knife under the bench as P16 enters mumbling.]

P16: (*to ALEX*) Don't let them keep you down, man. They're always trying to keep you down. Stick it to the man. You gotta be free... (*etc.*)

[P16 exits. ALEX stares in the direction of P16. On the other side of the stage there is the sound of a group of protesters coming closer. They are yelling and chanting "Free Him" and are carrying signs. ALEX moves to the other side of the stage to get a look but is nearly run over by them as they pass through. Exhausted, ALEX returns to the bench. The dog sounds become more obvious.]

ALEX: Free him? Don't let them keep you down? What are you trying to tell me now?

YP2: (*runs on stage*) Hey you!

ALEX: Me?

YP2: Yeah, you. Can you help?

ALEX: I don't know. I...

YP2: There's a dog over there who's been there for a very long time. She's tied up. I think she's trying to get free. She's starving and she's gonna get hurt. Can you help her? Please! Please!

ALEX: Well, I don't know.

YP2: C,mon. She needs help real bad.

ALEX: You sure she doesn't belong to someone?

YP2: I don't know. She's been there a long time. No one should treat an animal like that. C'mon!

[YP2 takes ALEX by the hand and begins to drag him offstage but ALEX suddenly stops.]

ALEX: Wait!

[ALEX goes to the bench and recovers the knife.]

ALEX: We might need this to set her free.

[ALEX and YP2 go offstage. There is the sound of barking. After a moment ALEX returns to the stage with THE DOG.]

ALEX: (*to THE DOG*) Ah! There you go. You should feel a lot better now. We'll get you something to eat and get you all fixed up. Then, we'll figure out what happened here but I think you and I might be spending a lot of time together. It's you and me now.

[ALEX pets THE DOG for a few moments]

ALEX: OK. Let's go. (*on the way out*) This really is a lucky day!

[ALEX and THE DOG exit together]

Curtain

Property List:

stage knife

dog leash or rope

From The House

A Ten-Minute Comedy

Cast

PERSON 1 (P1) - a theater goer.

PERSON 2 (P2) - a theater goer.

PERSON 3 (P3) - a theater goer.

AUDIENCE MEMBER (AM) - Someone chosen from the audience.

Note 1: It would be helpful if all three characters could sing (or maybe not?). The song to sing is included below and is in the public domain though any song could be substituted for it.

Note 2: The parts can be played by persons of any gender or ethnicity. Pronouns may be changed as needed.

Note 3: This play might get a little messy.

Scene

An empty stage except for a row of seats down stage.

Time

The Present.

Script

[At rise, there is an empty row of seats. After a moment, P1

enters with a tub of popcorn. P1 acts as if it is challenging to get to the right seat which is near the middle. P1 sits down and stares at the audience with anticipation. After another moment, P1 waves off stage.]

P1: Hey! Over here!

[P2 and P3 enter each with their own tub of popcorn and sit in the seats next to P1.]

P2: Are you sure these are our seats?

P1: Well, I couldn't find any floor markers. It's too dark but I'm pretty sure these are ours. Should be up front.

P3: These are nice seats. How did you score them? Did you win the lottery or something?

P1: No. An old pal from high school called me up and said he could get these at a discount price. It was still a pretty penny. It's supposed to be a great show, though!

P2: Really? Your buddy from high school told you that?

P1: Well, yeah.

[P2 and P3 look at each other in doubt.]

P1: Oh, come on. It will be great. Just wait and see.

P2: (*takes a big bite of popcorn*) Well, at least the popcorn's good.

P3: What's it about?

P1: The popcorn?

P3: The play!

P1: Oh, I don't know. One of those angst ridden emotional roller coasters with important lessons for living together in the modern world. You know, that sort of thing.

P2: You have no idea, do you?

P1: Not a clue.

P3: A night to remember!

P1: Why don't you two just sit back and have an open mind?

P2: Whatever!

[P1, P2, and P3 sit and stare at the audience for a few moments in anticipation. The house lights go up just enough to see faces in the audience.]

P3: This is weird.

P1: What?

P3: This screen or curtain they have set up for the show.

P2: Yeah, weird. It looks like we're staring at a bunch of people.

P1: Probably one of those CGI screens. You know, computer generated images to make it look like there's a bunch of people staring at you.

P3: Why would they do that?

P1: Maybe it's part of the play. They're probably characters in the play.

[P1, P2, and P3 should improvise as they say things about people in the audience such as "Hey look at this one..." Nothing said should be in any way offensive or cruel but should be light hearted and funny.]

P2: They look incredibly real!

P1: Modern day technology.

P3: (*looks closer*) Maybe they ARE real!

P2: No way!

P1: OK! I'll tell you what. I'm going to throw a piece of popcorn at the supposedly REAL people on the screen. If any one of them can catch the popcorn, we will know they are real. But if they are not real, the popcorn will just bounce off. Yeah?

P3: Yeah!

P2: Go for it!

P1: (*stands and walks to the edge of the stage*) Now remember, if one of these fake people catches this, they are real.

[P1 throws single pieces of popcorn at willing participants in the audience. P2 and P3 quickly join in and do the same. Each time the popcorn misses the thrower says "Nope, not real." When someone finally manages to catch one, P1, P2, and P3 freeze in shock.]

P1: That one ate the popcorn.

P2: What?

P3: That means... they're real!

P2: Why are we sitting and staring at a bunch of real people?

P3: And what are they all doing on stage? Is this some kind of overblown musical?

[P1, P2, and P3 look at each other as if they are about to sing, then decide against it.]

P1: Umm... (*looks around*) I think we're the ones on stage!

P2: What? Are you kidding me?

P3: What kind of stupid tickets did you get, anyways?

P1: I don't know but I think they're expecting us to do something.

P2: What exactly are they expecting us to do?

P3: I don’t know. Maybe if we…

P1: (*rises dramatically and overacts*) To be or not to be. That is the question! Whether 'tis nobler in the mind to suffer the slings and arrows of outrageous fortune, or to take arms against a sea of troubles and by opposing end them…

P2: (*to P3*) What’s he doing?

P3: Shakespeare, I think.

P1: To die, to sleep, no more! And by a sleep we, uh, say to stop the heart and the shock of flesh that our heirs cause us when we wish for consummation…

P3: (*to P2*) You sure that’s Shakespeare?

P2: Barely!

P1: (*continues*) To die! To sleep! What is there to rub? (*pulls out a pocket knife*) For in that, uh, hangover, what dreams coil up and do a little shuffle? And here I pause… (*opens the pocket knife*) For I would bear the whips and scorns of time…

P3: What’s he yammering on about?

P2: It’s a soliloquy about someone who’s thinking about taking his own life.

P3: What?

P1: (*continues*) The oppressors wrong, the proud man’s tummy! (*raises the pocket knife*)

P3: (*to P2*) What’s he doing now?

P2: Getting carried away.

P1: (*continues*) And a whole bunch of other terrible rotten things like, I think, some pits in a moment. And with this they, uh, regard the names of those who take action! (*moves to stab himself*)

[P1 and P2 intervene to stop P1]

P2: Whoa! Hold on there!

P3: Easy there!

[P2 and P3 ease P1 to a chair.]

P1: (*flustered*) Oh, I don't know what came over me.

P2: I'd say a case of bad drama to the head.

P1: (*points wearily to the audience*) But, they're still here and they expect a show.

P3: A show? (*to P2*) What are we going to do?

[Again, P1, P2, and P3 prepare to sing together then change their minds.]

P2: (*thinks*) I've got it. I used to do a little magic in college.

P3: Magic?

P2: Yea, it's easy. (*points to some chairs*) You just lie down on these chairs.

P3: These chairs?

P2: Yeah. Just lie down on your back and I'll do the rest.

P3: (*lies down*) OK. Just like this?

P2: Perfect. (*comes around behind P3 then speaks to the audience*) Honorable members of the audience, I present to you one of the most mesmerizing and difficult magic tricks ever performed.

P3: (*to P2*) You did this in college?

P2: (*aside*) Yeah. Don't worry. All I need is a... (*looks around*)

P1: All you need is a what?

P2: A saw.

P3: (*rises up suddenly*) A saw?

P2: (*pushes P3 back down*) Relax! It's just a trick!

P1: (*hands P2 the pocket knife*) Will this do?

P2: (*takes the knife*) It might. Let's see... (*raises the knife above P2's stomach*) (*to audience*) Now watch carefully as I cut this lovely young assistant into two pieces.

P3: (*stops P2*) Oh no you don't. This lovely young assistant is done and so is your magic trick.

P2: What? It would have worked.

P1: Did it work in college?

P2: I don't like to talk about that...

P3: Put that knife away.

P2: (*takes the knife, folds it, and puts it away*) Well, what do we do now? THEY (*points to the audience*) are still there.

P1: (*thinks*) Well, there's really only one thing left that can be done.

[P1 looks back and forth to P2 and P3 until they realize the idea.]

P2: Oh no! Not that!

P3: Come on! You've got to come up with something else beside that.

P2: Come on! It's time for the big closer. All we need is...

ALL: (*turns to the audience*) A willing volunteer!

[P2 and P3 go into the audience and find someone (AM) to bring on stage. The AM is seated in one of the chairs and faces the audience. The actors should improvise a little by doing things such as asking the AM for their name and to try and make them feel comfortable.]

P1: I bet you wondered why we chose you, don't you. (*AM may respond*) Well... (*singing*) It had to be you, it had to be you...

P2: (*singing*) We wandered around and finally found the somebody who...

P3: (*singing*) Could make us be true, could make us be blue, and even glad just to know you.

ALL: (*singing*) It had to be you, wonderful you, it had to be you.

[More to the musical production can be improvised including a possible kick line. After, P1 thanks the AM and escorts them back to their seat. P1, P2, and P3 all sit together exhausted in their seats. The house lights go down.]

P3: Well, that was something, wasn't it?

P1: Sure was.

P2: (*sits and thinks*) You know, I still don't get it. Are we the audience or are we the show?

P3: Maybe it's an experimental play about blurring the lines between the audience and the actors.

P2: Hmm! A study on the relationship between players and watchers.

P1: Sounds voyeuristic!

P3: The audience effect!

P2: The what?

P3: The audience effect: a study on how the presence of others influences one's actions.

P2: Well, I thought we acted great!

[ALL agree]

P3: (*to P1*) You know, I think you were right.

P1: About what?

P3: The play!

P1: What are you talking about?

P2: Oh right! What did you say? It was an angry rotten... I don't remember.

P3: He said it was an angst ridden emotional roller coaster with important lessons...

ALL: For living together in the modern world!

P1: I did say that, didn't I?

P2: You did and you could be right!

P3: You might even say it was a very profound experience!

[P1, P2, and P3 sit and ponder the thought for a few moments with nodding and hmms and expressions of approval, then...]

ALL: Naw!!

P3: (*to P1*) I think you just brought us to the wrong theater or something.

P2: (*to P3 pointing to P1*) No. This was another one of their practical jokes.

P1: Umm, yeah. A practical joke. That's it! All for the sake of good fun. But you have to admit it was a good play, though,huh?

P3: Not bad.

P2: Better than that one you brought us to last month.

P3: Yeah. The actors just stared at each other for an hour until the audience got fed up and started throwing popcorn at them.

P1: (*pointing to audience*) Just like those people out there?

[P1, P2, and P3 throw popcorn at each other and at the audience then start to make their way offstage making comments as they go. They finally exit]

Curtain

Property List:

- Three large tubs of popcorn
- Pocket knife

Grandma's House

A Ten-Minute Comedy

Cast

LUCINDA - AKA "Little Red Riding Hood" is a woman who wears a red cape.

HANSEL - A boy who speaks with an accent (not necessarily German).

GRETEL - A girl who speaks with a similar accent.

GRANDMA - an elderly woman.

WOLF - A frightening character possibly in a wolf costume holding a notebook and carrying a "grandma" dress.

Note: The parts can be played by persons of any gender or ethnicity. Pronouns may be changed as needed.

Scene

A cottage in the woods. Can include simple furniture including at least two or three chairs and a table. On the table is a tube of Super Glue with the cap off.There needs to be a door on one side of the stage that allows the audience to see on both sides.

Time

Once upon a time.

Script

[At rise, HANSEL and GRETEL are seated in chairs inside the house. They have been glued to the seats and are trying to escape.]

HANSEL: I'm stuck!

GRETEL: I can't get out of this chair. I told you we shouldn't come here.

HANSEL: You said there'd be candy here.

GRETEL: I didn't say that we should just break in to get it.

HANSEL: Well, how else are we going to get it? You know SHE isn't going to just give us some.

GRETEL: And what happens when SHE gets back? She's going to have us for dinner.

HANSEL: We've gotta get out of these chairs.

GRETEL: What kind of cruel person thinks to put glue on the seats?

HANSEL: An evil mastermind, that's who!

GRETEL: Maybe we should just start screaming for help. (*starts to open her mouth*)

HANSEL: No, don't! SHE might hear you.

GRETEL: Oh yeah. What are we going to do?

[LUCINDA enters through the door and sees the two children. Both LUCINDA and the children take turns screaming in fear at each other. Feel free to improvise.]

LUCINDA: Are you here to rob me?

HANSEL: Rob you? Can't you see we are glued to these chairs? How are we supposed to rob you?

LUCINDA: Why are you glued to the chairs?

GRETEL: What? Do you think we did this to ourselves?

LUCINDA: How would I know and why did you scream at me?

HANSEL: Because you're the....

GRETEL: Yeah, you're the...

LUCINDA: I'm the what?

HANSEL and GRETEL: The Wicked One!

LUCINDA: The what? Oh, come on. Do I look wicked?

HANSEL: Well, no, but...

GRETEL: You could be in disguise.

LUCINDA: For goodness sake! I am no Wicked One. Now, calm down and tell me what happened.

HANSEL: Well, we found this AirBnB that was supposed to have lots of candy.

GRETEL: So we decided to check it out.

LUCINDA: You mean you decided to break in!

HANSEL: What do you want from us? We got helicopter parents and need to boost our own self esteem!

LUCINDA: (*mockingly*) Really? But what is all this about a Wicked One?

GRETEL: Well, there were a couple of Yelp reviews about his place that mentioned the presence of an evil grandmother but we just thought those were from angry reviewers.

HANSEL: Until we found ourselves caught in her trap of glued chairs. We thought you were her.

LUCINDA: I came here to see MY grandma but I can assure you she's not evil.

GRETEL: Oh yeah? Then why does she lure little children here with candy?

LUCINDA: My grandma does not lure children here. Besides, she's diabetic. Look around. You see any candy here?

[LUCINDA waves her hand around the room. HANSEL and GRETEL do not see any candy and shake their heads.]

LUCINDA: My grandma is a sweet lady who wouldn't hurt anyone. So just relax.

HANSEL: OK, OK. So, how are you going to get us out of here?

LUCINDA: Let me see what I can find to get you off those chairs.

[LUCINDA looks around the house for a tool for prying the kids off the chairs. As she looks...]

LUCINDA: By the way, what do I call you two?

GRETEL: I'm Gretel.

HANSEL: And I'm Hansel.

LUCINDA: Oh, good. Gretel and Hansel. I bet your parents are all worried about you. We'll just get you two out of those chairs and then... (*freezes*) Wait a minute! Gretel and Hansel. Hansel and Gretel! You're Hansel and Gretel?

HANSEL: I'm Hansel.

GRETEL: And I'm Gretel.

LUCINDA: (*moves closer to the children*) Don't you know about your own story?

[HANSEL and GRETEL look at each other then look back

at LUCINDA]

HANSEL and GRETEL: No.

LUCINDA: You were right to be worried about the Wicked One. You are being hunted as we speak but you must have come to the wrong house. (*still looking for a tool*) We have to get you out of here and send you home to safety.

[LUCINDA continues to look but can't find anything except knitting tools.]

HANSEL: You never told us your name.

LUCINDA: Oh well, yes. My name is Lucinda but people sometimes call me Little Red Riding Hood because I always wear this lovely cape. (*shows off her cape*)

GRETEL: Did you say Little Red...

HANSEL: Riding Hood?

LUCINDA: Why, yes.

[HANSEL and GRETEL cover their mouths and gasp]

GRETEL: Don't you know YOUR story?

LUCINDA: MY story?

HANSEL: Yes. You are going to be visited by a hungry horrible wolf who will disguise himself as your grandmother and then...

LUCINDA: And then, what?

GRETEL: He's going to eat you.

[Everyone screams.]

LUCINDA: (*calms everyone down*) OK, OK. Let's just calm down. We can figure out a way for all of us to get out of this. We just need to think.

[Suddenly GRANDMA enters through the door. When the door is open, LUCINDA, HANSEL, and GRETEL start screaming again. Eventually GRANDMA gets their attention.]

GRANDMA: What is going on here?

GRETEL: Are you the Wicked One?

HANSEL: Are you the Evil One?

LUCINDA: Are you the Hungry Wolf?

GRANDMA: Oh my goodness, no! (*to LUCINDA*) I'm your grandmother. *(to HANSEL and GRETEL*) And the most evil thing I have ever done is refuse to tip the Self Checkout Machine at the grocery store. Maybe this will help... (*goes to get a very large clearly marked container of candy*) Here you go. (*gives some candy to HANSEL and GRETEL*)

GRETEL: I told you there was candy here.

LUCINDA: (*to GRANDMA*) I thought you were diabetic.

GRANDMA: Oh, I always keep a little on hand for guests. (*to HANSEL and GRETEL*) And who are you two?

HANSEL: I'm Hansel

GRETEL: And I'm Gretel.

GRANDMA: And what are they doing stuck to my chairs?

LUCINDA: They came to steal your candy.

GRANDMA: Is that so? Oh yeah? Well, we'll see about that!

[GRANDMA pulls a large crowbar out of a hidden location and approaches the children. Upon seeing GRANDMA approach them, the children start screaming again.]

LUCINDA: Grandma! Don't hurt them!

GRANDMA: Hurt them? Oh, don't be ridiculous. I'm not going to hurt them. I'm going to set them free.

[GRANDMA goes to the children, puts the crowbar behind them, and wrenches them free from the seats with some struggle. Feel free to improvise.]

HANSEL: Thank you!

GRETEL: Yes, thank you.

GRANDMA: Oh, you're welcome. (*sees Super Glue*) Oh, goodness me. I always forget to put the cap back on that Super Glue.

[GRANDMA puts the cap on the glue then puts the glue in her pocket. The children run to GRANDMA and GRANDMA hugs them. Then there is a knock at the door; Everyone gasps.]

LUCINDA: Who is it?

WOLF: (*from behind the door with an open notebook and dress in hand*) Pizza delivery.

LUCINDA: We didn't order any pizza.

WOLF: (*shuffles pages*) Uh, special delivery.

GRANDMA: The mail doesn't come out this way.

WOLF: (*shuffles pages*) Uh, yeah. That's right. I'm afraid I'm lost. Could I come in please and, uh, use your… phone?

GRANDMA: Go away!

WOLF: Are you sure you can't let me in? Not by the hair of your chiny-chin chin?

HANSEL and GRETEL and GRANDMA and LUCINDA: No!

GRANDMA: And you leave my facial hair out of this!

WOLF: Then I will have to huff and puff and BLOW your house down!

GRETEL: Look, buddy! You've got the wrong story. There are no pigs here.

WOLF: What? (*shuffles pages*) It's got to be here somewhere. Ah! (*puts on the dress and speaks in a high pitched voice*) Could I speak to the exclusive proprietor of this fine establishment, please?

GRANDMA: Oh, why certainly! (*opens the door*)

LUCINDA: Grandma!

[THE WOLF walks in still reading from the notebook.]

HANSEL: No! It's the Wicked One!

WOLF: Oh, no, no, no. Not me. I am a most gentle and gentile geriatric.

LUCINDA: Who are you?

WOLF: (*to LUCINDA*) Oh, my dear! You're Little Red Riding Hood aren't you? Don't you recognize me? I'm your sweet and kind Grand... (*looks at GRANDMA then flips pages*) Uh, Great Aunt. Yes. I'm your great Aunt Lupie!

LUCINDA: I don't have a great Aunt Lupie.

WOLF: Of course you do, dear. Check your Twenty Three and Me results. You'd be surprised what shows up.

LUCINDA: You can say that again!

WOLF: Then come along with me so I can get you back home and cook you, I mean cook you a fine dinner. Doesn't that sound nice? (*heads toward LUCINDA*)

GRANDMA: Just a moment!

WOLF: What?

GRANDMA: What's with the script?

WOLF: Script? No. I'm just trying to catch up on some reading.

GRANDMA: You're new at this aren't you?

WOLF: Well, I, uh...

GRANDMA: C'mon. I get it. You got tired of chasing rabbits and squirrels and so you went on YouTube and found out how to track down kids in red capes.

GRETEL: That's just plain sick!

GRANDMA: Then you downloaded the script and thought you could just improvise your way through it.

LUCINDA: Amateur! Next thing you know you'll be doing ten-minute plays in some backwater theater.

WOLF: I much prefer musicals.

[HANSEL and GRETEL begin singing and dancing their favorite musicals in their own accents.]

GRANDMA: (*calms down the children*) Children, please! Come sit down.

[GRANDMA motions toward the two chairs where the children were stuck before. The children move toward it.]

GRANDMA: Oh, not over there. (*points somewhere else*) Sit over there.

LUCINDA: Maybe you shouldn't have given them so much candy!

WOLF: (*reaches for LUCINDA's arm*) OK, missie. It's time to come home with your Auntie!

GRANDMA: (*cuts THE WOLF off from LUCINDA*) Just a moment there.

WOLF: What is it? We need to get back in time for my... uh, our dinner. (to LUCINDA) You must be getting hungry, dear. I know I am!

GRANDMA: You really are bad at this!

WOLF: What do you mean?

GRANDMA: You missed a whole section of the script.

WOLF: What? No I didn't.

HANSEL: Yeah, you did. What about the whole "My, what big ears you have!" bit, huh?

WOLF: (*flipping through pages*) What?

GRETEL: Yeah, and the "My, what big teeth you have!" thing. What about that, huh?

WOLF: (*still flipping through pages*) When was I supposed to say that?

GRANDMA: Here! Let me help you. It's right here. (p*oints to a place in the notebook*)

WOLF: What? I don't see it.

GRANDMA: Let me get my highlighter and show you.

[GRANDMA takes the Super Glue out of her pocket, takes off the cap, and then squeezes it onto the notebook paper.]

GRANDMA: There! You see it now?

WOLF: No!

GRANDMA: Then take a closer look.

[GRANDMA slams the notebook onto THE WOLF's

forehead until it is stuck and THE WOLF is covered by the notebook.]

WOLF: Hey! I can't see anything!

GRANDMA: Right this way.

[GRANDMA kicks THE WOLF out the door and closes it. Everyone celebrates.]

GRANDMA: Now that the Big Bad Wolf is gone. We can all relax. (*to LUCINDA*) Why don't you take these nice kids out to the zoo and see some NICE animals?

LUCINDA: OK! C'mon kids.

[HANSEL and GRETEL express their glee as they grab some more candy and exit with LUCINDA. GRANDMA walks around the room and straightens up for a bit.]

GRANDMA: Oh, this place is always a mess. I think I need to downsize. I heard there's a lovely one bedroom shoe for sale.

[GRANDMA exits]

Curtain

Property List:

- Two chairs
- Crowbar
- Candy
- Candy container (large)
- Notebook
- Something that looks like a tube of Super Glue with a cap

Left Behind

A Ten-Minute Comedy

Cast

FRANK - (m) a company employee for many years.

JERI - (f) a company employee for several years.

CHRIS - (m) a new company employee.

SERVER - the server for the pub.

Note: The parts can be played by persons of any gender or ethnicity. Pronouns may be changed as needed.

Scene

A local pub and eatery. There is a table with three chairs, center stage. The table has single page menus. Typical pub sounds are heard in the background.

Time

Present.

Script

[At rise, FRANK and JERI are seated at the table. They are looking over the menus.]

JERI: I don't even know why we bother looking at these menus. We get the same thing everytime.

FRANK: Something to do until we order, I guess.

JERI: Looks like they're having a special on meatloaf tonight?

FRANK: Have you had their meatloaf?

JERI: No.

FRANK: Nothing special about it. Stick to what you know.

JERI: Spicy Buffalo Wings From Hell it is. (*sets down the menu*)

FRANK: That way the burn covers the taste and you have a good excuse to drink more beer. (*sets down the menu*)

JERI: (*looks around*) That's IF we can get some service here. (*waves hand*) Over here! We're cheap but our money's still good. (*a beat*) Hey! Didn't you say you invited someone else here tonight?

FRANK: Yeah, the new guy. Started last week. Thought he should meet some of the crew. (*sees CHRIS*) Oh wait! There he is now. (*waves*) Over here!

[*CHRIS approaches the table and introduces himself. They shake hands and CHRIS sits down.*]

JERI: New guy, huh?

CHRIS: Yeah. Started last week.

FRANK: Takes a while to fit in. Don't worry, you'll settle in. (*to JERI*) Chris here is a bit of a genius. He came from the firm across town where I guess he did a bang-up job. We snatched him right up.

JERI: Is that so?

CHRIS: It's just talk.

[*The SERVER enters with a notepad.*]

SERVER: What can I get ya?

FRANK: Buffalo wings.

JERI: Buffalo wings.

CHRIS: (*picks up a menu*) What's good here?

SERVER: Well, we do have a special on...

FRANK: He'll have the Buffalo wings. (*to CHRIS*) Trust me!

SERVER: And three beers. (*all nod approvingly*) Got it! (*exits*)

JERI: So, Chris? How do you like it so far?

CHRIS: It's good. It's quite a challenge because it seems like there's so much to learn and get used to but I'll get it.

FRANK: Oh, yeah. You'll get it. All you need to remember for right now is to keep your distance from Marty.

CHRIS: Marty?

JERI: Oh yeah. Marty. Sometimes we call him Dopey?

CHRIS: Why?

FRANK: One ear is lower than the other. Kind of creepy.

JERI: Try not to stare.

FRANK: Can't trust people like that.

CHRIS: You can't?

[*The SERVER returns with three filled glasses and puts them on the table, then leaves.*]

JERI: It just ain't normal. That's all I'm saying.

CHRIS: But...

FRANK: Oh, forget about that. Let's drink to new beginnings, shall we?

[*FRANK, JERI, and CHRIS raise their glasses. FRANK and JERI hold their glass with their right hand. CHRIS holds his glass with his left hand. They all start to say "To new beginnings!" but only CHRIS finishes the phrase and starts to drink. FRANK and JERI freeze in mid-sentence as they watch CHRIS drink with his left hand. CHRIS takes a sip and then notices FRANK and JERI staring at him with a look of concern.*]

CHRIS: What? What did I do?

FRANK: Uh, nothing. It's nothing.

[*FRANK puts his hand on CHRIS' left arm and gently brings it down as if to hide it.*]

JERI: Yeah. It's nothing. Absolutely nothing.

CHRIS: Oh, come on. You both look like I just shot your dog or something.

JERI: You're a... (*looks at CHRIS' left hand*)

CHRIS: A what?

[*JERI holds up his left hand and shakes it while giving a dumb expression.*]

CHRIS: A Leftie?

[*Just as CHRIS says the word "leftie", JERI holds a finger to his lips as if to shush CHRIS while FRANK talks over CHRIS in an effort to cover up the word.*]

FRANK: (*to someone in the distance*) Hey! Good to see you. How have you been? How are the kids? Don't have any kids? Oh, right. You're mother? Oh, I'm sorry. Hey! Good talk! (*back to CHRIS*) Will you hold it down?

CHRIS: What's the problem here? Is this all because I use my le... (*FRANK and JERI give him a stern look*) Because I use my

OTHER hand?

FRANK: (*looks around*) You need to keep something like that to yourself. You could lose your job.

CHRIS: What?

JERI: Look! We're just trying to be your friends here. You just can't go around using that hand like that. It's... well, it's just not normal.

CHRIS: You're kidding , right? This is some kind of joke. I mean it's the twenty-first century, after all. Surely we're beyond...

FRANK: Look, pal. This could be the twenty-fifth century for all that matters. There are just some things people cannot abide in the name of decency.

CHRIS: Decency? I'm no different than either of you.

JERI: (*holds up left hand and shakes it*) Well, clearly that's not the case.

FRANK: (*to CHRIS*) You need to examine your choices in life if you expect to get any further in your career.

CHRIS: My choices?

FRANK: The hand you use may determine your future.

CHRIS: I didn't CHOOSE to be left-handed. I was BORN this way.

JERI: You really expect us to believe that?

CHRIS: I don't care what you believe. It's true, regardless. I was born with a dominant left hand.

FRANK: Haven't you ever heard the words: A wise man's heart is at his right hand; but a fool's heart is at his left?

JERI: Shakespeare?

FRANK: The Bible. Ecclesiastes.

CHRIS: You do know that the human heart sits partly to the LEFT of the body, don't you?

JERI: Blasphemy!

FRANK: (*leans in*) I know of a place that can help you out with your problem.

CHRIS: I don't have a...

FRANK: They will take you in for one month. You can say you have a medical condition or you need to go to rehab, it doesn't matter. That way the company will pay for it. They can teach you to use your right hand.

CHRIS: I don't need training. I can use my left hand just fine.

JERI: I hear they serve a nice lunch there.

CHRIS: I don't need a nice lunch. I need you two to let go of this...

FRANK: Hey! You don't have to worry about us. Others may want nothing to do with you but we're not like that. Others may be ignorant and intolerant but we're just not like that.

JERI: Yeah. We ain't no ignorant folk.

CHRIS: (*mockingly*) Good to know.

JERI: We're better than that.

FRANK: We know it's not your fault.

CHRIS: That's what I've been trying to tell you.

FRANK: It happens when you're very young. You see someone using their left hand and you think that's how it should be or you're repressed, or abused, or who knows?

CHRIS: What?

JERI: So sad.

FRANK: Your whole world gets turned around until you don't know what's right. It's only natural that you turn the wrong way.

JERI: So very sad.

CHRIS: What's sad is you two! My childhood was just fine. I had great parents and good friends and...

JERI: (*under the breath*) Probably all lefties!

FRANK: Probably a whole community of 'em.

CHRIS: That's enough of this. Clearly neither one of you is capable of understanding... (*starts to leave*)

FRANK: (*stops CHRIS*) No! You don't understand. You're, uh, *condition*, if allowed to spread could have grave consequences on the fabric of the society.

JERI: Grave consequences!

CHRIS: What are you talking about?

FRANK: Do you realize what would happen if more and more people became, you know, like you?

[*JERI lifts his left hand and shakes it menacingly in the air. FRANK nods in JERI's direction.*]

FRANK: The world's tools, computer keyboards, office furniture, musical instruments...

JERI: Golf clubs.

FRANK: Not to mention the entire system of writing in the Western world would be devastated. Everything would have to be re-fitted and redesigned. Machinery around the world would go idle and fall into disrepair. The economic impact alone would be catastrophic.

JERI: The end of civilization as we know it.

CHRIS: (*sits in disbelief*) I see. I had no idea.

FRANK: Well, pal. That's what we're here for. We want to try and...

CHRIS: I had no idea people could be so horribly ignorant.

JERI: Oh come on. Don't be so upset. The light of truth can be shocking.

CHRIS: Especially when you remain in the dark, apparently.

JERI: What?

FRANK: The Boston Strangler, Jack The Ripper, John Dillinger, Billy the Kid.

CHRIS: Friends of yours?

FRANK: All lefties.

JERI: Hitler.

CHRIS: Adolph Hitler was not left handed.

JERI: You sure? He may have just been good at hiding it.

CHRIS: How about Albert Einstein, Mahatma Gandhi, and Leonardo DaVinci? All lefties.

JERI: And yet they found ways to overcome their affliction.

CHRIS: (*stands*) OK. That's enough.

FRANK: Wait! We're sorry.We really didn't mean anything. We were just concerned, is all. We want you to do well at the firm. To start off on the right foot, so to speak.

JERI: Or the right HAND.

FRANK: We all have certain conditions we have to overcome. I got big feet.

JERI: Yeah and I have this hairy mole right in the middle of my... (*stands and starts to point toward bum*)

FRANK: (*stops JERI*) We don't need to know about that.

JERI: I was just trying to... (*sits*)

FRANK: (*to JERI*) I know what you was trying to do. This is about Chris, not your fleshy protrusions. (*to CHRIS*) Look! The point is that you're our new buddy. And at this firm we look out for each other. We help each other. We just want you to do well so we can stay together and hang out like we're doing now.

JERI: Yeah. We don't care what you do on your own time. What you do with your left hand is your business. A lot of my friends have left hands.

FRANK: We're just trying to look out for you.

CHRIS: (*thinks for a moment*) OK. I'll tell you what. You both promise to never, ever bring this subject up again and I'll forget all about this incident. Can you do that?

FRANK: Yeah, sure. I can do that. The topic will never cross my lips again.

CHRIS: (*to JERI*) And you?

JERI: Yeah sure. (*pulls finger across lips*) Mum's the word.

CHRIS: Fine! It's settled. No more talk about hands.

FRANK: (*slaps hand on table*) Now there's something I can drink to.

[CHRIS consciously and conspicuously picks up his glass and lifts it with his right hand and lifts it into the air.

CHRIS: No hands!

FRANK: (*lifts glass with right hand*) No hands!

JERI: (*unconsciously lifts glass with left hand*) No hands!

[JERI lifts the glass to his lips. CHRIS and FRANK stare at him. JERI takes a sip, puts down the glass then wipes his lips.]

JERI: (*noticing the others staring at him*) What?

<u>Curtain</u>

Property List:

- Table
- Three chairs
- Three filled glasses
- Three single page menus

Lost In Translation

A Ten-Minute Comedy

Cast

SAM - a job seeker looking for adventure in another country. Wears a suit.

VASILIS - a translator. Speaks with a heavy foreign sounding accent. Wears casual clothing.

Note 1: The origin of the accent can be from anywhere. The name of the character and the country should be changed to fit the origin.

Note 2: The parts can be played by persons of any gender or ethnicity. Pronouns may be changed as needed.

Scene

An office setting with chairs and a table. The chairs should face each other so that the audience can see both faces. There is a door or the impression of a door at the side.

Time

Present.

Script

[At rise, VASILIS is seated at the table reading something or is on his phone. After a moment, SAM knocks on the door then enters.]

VASILIS: (*in a heavy accent*) Ah! Good morning, good morning. Come on in, please.

SAM: Thank you.

VASILIS: Have seat. (*gestures toward seat*) You are here for interview, yes?

SAM: Yes.

VASILIS: Oh good, good. Sit, please. (*sits*) Now, I tell you how this works. I call company, they ask me questions, then I ask you questions. You give me answers and then I translate back to company, yes?

SAM: OK.

VASILIS: OK. We off to a good start. You ready?

SAM: (*takes a breath*) Yes. I think so.

VASILIS: OK. We go now.

[*VASILIS picks up a cell phone and dials a number while reading from a piece of paper. He begins talking into the phone. During the entire conversation both with SAM and on the phone, VASILIS speaks English but with a very heavy accent. SAM gets suspicious as the conversation progresses.*]

VASILIS: (*on phone*) Yes... Hello... This is Ajax Company? Yes, yes. We are ready to begin interview... (*nods at SAM*) Yes, yes.... Understood... OK. I tell him. (*to SAM*) They are ready now. What is your full name?

SAM: Samuel Schlossheimer.

VASILIS: His name is...

[*The actors are encouraged to improvise on getting VASILIS to correctly pronounce SAM's full name.*]

VASILIS: Current address?

SAM: Yorba Linda, California.

[*VASILIS gives SAM a look and then another round of improvisation begins on the name of the town until...*]

SAM: L.A. Just say L.A.

VASILIS: Oh, that is better. (*on phone*) He lives in L.A. (*to SAM*) And you are ok to move to [Greece] to work for this company?

SAM: Yes.

VASILIS: (*on phone*) Yes he move. (*to SAM*) But you do not speak [Greek], correct?

SAM: That is correct.

VASILIS: (*to phone*) Not [Greek]. We are ready for next question. (*pause*)

SAM: Um, excuse me.

[*VASILIS holds up one finger as if to say "wait*]

SAM: Excuse me. I need to ask you a question.

VASILIS: (*to phone*) Just a moment. (*mutes phone and turns to SAM*) What is it? I'm trying to get next question. Is very important we not leave them waiting.

SAM: Yes, I understand but there's something I don't understand.

VASILIS: Yes?

SAM: Well, it sounds like you are just saying everything in English, just in a heavy accent.

VASILIS: Oh yeah. Well it is just a very specific dialect that comes from a very tiny village in very small part of the country. Long history, something about pirates and skirmishes and temporary occupations, a lot of boring stuff. Would take too long to explain. It is very difficult to learn and translate. Not many people can do it. You very lucky to have me.

SAM: Oh, I see.

VASILIS: Shall I continue?

SAM: Uh, yes.

VASILIS: (*unmutes phone*) He still alive. Next question. (*to SAM*) They want to know your work experience.

SAM: Well, I have worked at many high profile and significant firms all across the country.

VASILIS: (*to phone*) He says he can't keep a job. (*to SAM*) References?

SAM: Oh, I have excellent references and can get them to you within the next week.

VASILIS: (*to phone*) He say the check not come through yet for the people he hired to write references. (*to SAM*) How long you been doing this work?

SAM: Well, let's see. I started working out of college for maybe twenty, no twenty-five years. The years seem to fly by.

VASILIS: (*to phone*) He's old and a little bit senile. Next?

SAM: Wait a minute! That doesn't sound right.

VASILIS: (*to phone*) Please hold. Technical difficulty. (*to SAM*) You want to, how you say, sabotage this interview? You not want this job?

SAM: Of course I want this job. That is why I am here but it sounds like you are just twisting my words around in English.

VASILIS: I told you. Is difficult translation. You must just be patient and trust me. (*unmutes phone*) We are back. I am very sorry. (*to SAM*) They want to know about your sales records.

SAM: Sales records?

VASILIS: Yes. Very important.

SAM: Well, we naturally have undulating sales points with significant peaks and occasional troughs but overall our results are consistent.

VASILIS: (*to phone*) Mostly dreadful.

SAM: (*stands*) Now wait just a moment. I know what I heard. You are ruining my interview.

VASILIS: (*to phone*) Call back in five minutes. (*to SAM*) No, no. Is like I said. Very tricky. You must trust me. We get you the job of your dreams. Now, here.

[*VASILIS guides SAM back to his chair*]

VASILIS: You sit. Take it easy. (*SAM sits*) Good. Now you just relax. It is going very good. (*VASILIY sits*) I tell you what. You tell me a little about yourself and then I call them back and explain everything and things will be just fine, no?

SAM: Alright, alright. I guess I'm just a little nervous.

VASILIS: Of course. Here, let me get you a little water, eh? It is good to stay, how you say, hibernated? (*gets a glass of water*)

SAM: Hydrated.

VASILIS: high-rated?

SAM: HyDrated!

VASILIS: Oh, Drated like the singer?

SAM: No, that's Drake.

VASILIS: Hydraked? Sounds dirty.

SAM: No, it's... never mind. I'll take that glass of water.

[VASILIS gets a glass of water then walks toward SAM]

VASILIS: Yes, here you go. Nice cold water. Very refreshing. (*reaches SAM*) Oh my goodness! It has been five minutes.

[When VASILIS is just over SAM, he turns his wrist over to look at his watch which is also the same hand that is holding the water. The cold water goes into SAM's lap]

SAM: Whoah!

VASILIS: Oh, Mr. Schlotzenskimmer I am very sorry. This is just terrible. I have towels to dry you up. (*phone rings*) Oh, no. They have called back. Here!

[VASILIS grabs paper towels, runs back to SAM and starts patting him with the towels]

SAM: Answer... the... phone...

[SAM tries to talk but his mouth gets blocked by a towel. Eventually he stands and pushes VASILIS away]

VASILIS: (*finally realizing what SAM is saying*) Oh, yes. (*drops wet paper towel on floor*) I answer the phone. (*to phone*) Yes, hello? No, everything OK. Just needed a short bathroom break. We are fine. (*to SAM*) You ready to continue?

[As Sam attempts to return to his chair he slips on the paper towel but tries to retain his composure. As SAM struggles...]

SAM: No!

VASILIS: (*to phone*) Yes, yes. Everything OK. What is next question? (*pause*) Oh, OK. (*to SAM*) Example of your best and worst work day.

SAM: Best and worst work day?

VASILIS: Yes. Your best day. What happened? Why was it so good? Your worst day. Why so bad? You know.

SAM: (*gains composure*) Well, let's see. My best day was when we had our employees bring their kids to work and they got to see how everything worked and my worst day would have to be... (thinks) oh! When the toilets backed up in the company bathrooms.

VASILIS: (*to SAM*) Oh, yes. Very good. I see why you are good at this. (*to phone*) He say he in favor of child labor and he not able to keep his building properly maintained.

SAM: Now, wait a minute. You're not speaking in any kind of dialect and you are ruining this interview for me. You tell me what's going on right now or I'm going to have you arrested for fraud.

VASILIS: (*to phone*) Uh, I call you right back. He has to use the bathroom again. There may be a medical issue. (*hangs up then to SAM*) Please don't call the police. I am poor immigrant...

SAM: (*thinks about doing something rash but then reconsiders*) Now you're going to sit down right there and I'm going to sit down here and then you're going to tell me exactly what's going on.

VASILIS: OK, OK. I tell you... I was born in a small village in a remote town... We were very poor. My entire family: my mama and my papa and the twelve children and all our grandparents and all the children who no one knew where they came from and all the cousins and the nephews and the nieces and the neighbors and the peddlers on the streets had to work hard to keep food on the table...

[As VASILIS talks, melancholic music, preferably from the same origin as his accent, begins to play. VASILIS pretends not to hear it but SAM hears it and gets confused.]

SAM: What is that music?

VASILIS: (*continues*) We had to toil from sunup to sundown, through all kinds of weather. There was no time for play or fun. We couldn't throw the ball or chase the other stick like other kids. There was no time for our parents to tell us bedtime stories or tales about our ancestors...

SAM: Could you turn that music down?

[As VASILIS continues to talk, there is the sound of a cat, then a dog barking, then lightning and rain and the lights flicker. Throughout these changes SAM looks around confused but does not get angry. Eventually he just gives up and collapses in his seat.]

VASILIS: It was then that I knew I had to do something different, something drastic to change my life. So I left my little hometown even though my mother cried and my father cried and the twelve children and the grandparents and the cousins and the nephews and the nieces and all the neighbors and the peddlers cried. I left the little town I had known all my life and went to America so I could learn English and be a translator. I studied and I learned and I toiled and then I got my paper that says I am good English speaker. I brought my paper back to my country and showed my sisters and brothers and cousins and nephews and nieces and the neighbors and the street sellers and they all became really happy for me. So I came back to America to find work...

[Suddenly, the sounds stop and the lights return to normal. VASILIY stops talking. SAM looks around dazed]

SAM: What just happened? No music, No dog? No cat? No rain and thunder?

[*VASILIS walks over to SAM and takes his hand. When he talks to SAM he no longer has a foreign accent*]

VASILIS: Congratulations, Mr. Sclossheimer from Yorba Linda, California.

SAM: (*looks shocked*) What?

VASILIS: You have successfully completed your interview and we are happy to say that we would like to offer you the position.

SAM: I, uh, I don't understand.

VASILIS: You see, our executives are constantly under a great deal of pressure. As much as we are interested in your credentials we also need to know how you act under extreme conditions of stress. You did not incite violence and were able, for the most part, to maintain your self-control.

SAM: I did?

VASILIS: Ah you see? You are humble as well. (*shakes hand again*) Congratulations. We will see you Monday morning, yes?

SAM: Well, uh, yes. Monday morning.

VASILIS: Good, good. (*guides SAM to the door*) Someone will show you where to go to sign the paperwork and then you will be all set.

SAM: Uh, thank you.

VASILIS: Oh no, thank you. We always need good employees. Bye now.

[*VASILIS leads SAM through the door. He then returns to the desk and straightens up. In a few moments there is a knock at the door. VASILIS goes to the door and opens it. He then speaks in a completely different accent.*]

VASILIS: Yah! Come in! I will be your translator.

Curtain

Property List:

- Door
- Table
- Two chairs
- Cellphone
- Laptop or notepad and pen
- Glass
- Water
- Paper towels

October Seventh

A Ten Minute Drama

Cast

JORDAN - a young male dressed for a casual date

EMILY - a young female dressed for a casual date

SERVER - the one who takes their food order.

Note: The roles can be played by persons of any ethnicity or gender. The pronouns should be changed as needed.

Scene

A small cafe or restaurant. There is a table with two chairs across from each other. On the table are some plates, utensils, and glasses and menus. There are two mugs. There can be some food on the plates. EMILY is wearing a ring.

Time

The Present.

Script

[*At rise, JORDAN and EMILY sit across from each other*

at a small table looking a little uncomfortable. After a moment, the SERVER enters.]

SERVER: Welcome! Can I start you both off with a cup of coffee this morning?

EMILY: Oh, coffee would be wonderful.

SERVER: Cream and sugar?

EMILY: Yes.

JORDAN: For me as well but I take it black.

SERVER: Very good. I'll be right back with those coffees. (*exits*)

EMILY: (*picks up a menu*) What's good here?

JORDAN: I heard the house made doughnuts are amazing.

EMILY: Doughnuts, huh?

JORDAN: Yeah. They're a game changer.

EMILY: Can't say no to that. (*nervously puts down her menu*) So...

JORDAN: So...

EMILY: I'm sorry. I'm just a little nervous. I've never really had one of these before.

JORDAN: An amazing doughnut?

EMILY: No. You know what I mean... an online date. You?

JORDAN: Online dating?

EMILY: Yeah.

JORDAN: A few times but I keep thinking I'm done with this whole app dating thing and then I decide to give it one more try.

EMILY: So you decided to give it another try with me?

JORDAN: That's right. There was just something about your profile that made me want to meet you.

EMILY: Oh, really? Like what?

JORDAN: You seemed to me to be someone who liked to walk her own trail, someone who wasn't afraid to be her own person, someone who cared about the world.

EMILY: You got all that from my profile?

JORDAN: I got all that from your picture. You have very kind eyes.

EMILY: Now you're snowballin' me.

JORDAN: No, really. You have a very gentle smile.

EMILY: So did Ted Bundy, apparently.

JORDAN: Are you a serial killer?

EMILY: (*picks up the knife and holds it menacingly*) That's right. A serial killer. (*laughs mockingly*)

[*The SERVER enters with two cups of coffee and sees EMILY holding a knife. She drops the coffee before getting to the table.*]

EMILY: (*to the SERVER*) Oh my goodness. I'm just, uh, play-acting. We're doing a part in a play. You know... short play, a comedy. Hah, hah?

SERVER: Oh, a play?

JORDAN: Yeah.

SERVER: OK. I'm sorry. I'll be right back with your coffee.

[*The SERVER picks up the cups and exits. EMILY and*

JORDAN look at each other and hold back a laugh.]]

JORDAN: So, not a serial killer?

EMILY: No, are you?

JORDAN: Not even close.

EMILY: Well, at least we got that out of the way. So… (*glances at her phone then looks back up*) Jordan, tell me a little about yourself.

JORDAN: I've followed a few different lines of work. I started out in printing, doing copies for small business owners who didn't know how to operate their machines. Then I did a little retail and spent some time in customer service.

EMILY: And now?

JORDAN: Now I work for a really great non-profit organization that works to get important news out to people in troubled parts of the world.

EMILY: Sounds exciting.

JORDAN: It is exciting. And fulfilling. What about you, what do you do?

EMILY: Oh, well, I'm a barista during the day but my real passion is in making jewelry.

JORDAN: Jewelry? That's fantastic. Do you have any samples of your work with you?

EMILY: (*removes a ring from her finger*) Here. I made this ring. (*hands the ring to JORDAN*)

JORDAN: (*looks at the ring*) It's beautiful. You're very talented.

[*JORDAN examines the ring as the SERVER returns and*

places the coffee on the table. JORDAN reaches across to return the ring to EMILY.]

SERVER: Here you go. (*sees the ring*) Oh my goodness. That's beautiful. May I see it?

[*JORDAN looks at EMILY for approval then hands the ring over to the SERVER.*]

SERVER: Lovely, just lovely. (*looks at both of them*) Is this part of the play or are you really going to propose to her?

JORDAN: Propose? Oh no, it's not... We just met.

EMILY: He's a little nervous. You can understand.

SERVER: Oh, of course. I understand. He moves fast. Let me get out of your way. (*returns the ring to JORDAN then starts to go*)

EMILY: No, wait. We need to order. These things always make me so hungry.

SERVER: (*stammering*) Oh, well, yes. I guess that makes sense. What would you like?

EMILY: I heard your doughnuts are amazing.

SERVER: Best in town. We bake them in-house. It takes some time to make but it's worth the wait.

EMILY: One chocolate glazed for me, then.

JORDAN: I'll have the same.

SERVER: Two doughnuts coming up but you should have plenty of time to... you know! (*to JORDAN in a half whisper*) Go get her, tiger! (*quickly exits*)

JORDAN: Did a little bit of acting in college, did you?

EMILY: How'd you guess?

JORDAN: (*looks at the ring again*) This really is stunning work.

EMILY: Oh, thanks. It's just a hobby.

JORDAN: Don't underestimate yourself. Some people turn hobbies into innovative businesses and inventions that have changed the world.

EMILY: Oh, come on. How can tinkering around in some basement ever lead to anything important?

JORDAN: Ever heard of Facebook? The personal computer? Mrs. Field's Cookies?

EMILY: They all just got lucky.

JORDAN: Luck, talent, skill, belief. It takes a combination of all these things–but mostly belief.

EMILY: Belief in what?

JORDAN: Mostly in yourself.

EMILY: Oh, I don't have much of that.

JORDAN: But, why not? You're talented, smart, beautiful, and creative. You just need to add a little fuel to the fire.

EMILY: How do I do that?

JORDAN: (*leans forward*) That's where the belief comes in–belief in your inner strength and abilities–belief that you can be something greater.

EMILY: How do I find a way to do that?

JORDAN: (*looking intently*) It helps to know that you are connected to something greater, something more... wonderful.

EMILY: Something greater? (*stares for a few moments*) You're not one of those, uh, bible thumpers are you?

JORDAN: (*leans back*) Who, me? Oh, no. (*beat*) It's just that I have been where you are now. I was once full of doubt. I didn't know what to do.

EMILY: (*picks up her coffee in thought*) Yeah. Sometimes it's like walking on the beach while trying to drag cement blocks behind you.

JORDAN: It's hard to know how to move forward.

EMILY: Yeah.

[*EMILY continues to look thoughtfully away. JORDAN stares at EMILY. After a moment EMILY notices.*]

EMILY: What? What is it? Do I have crumbs on my face?

JORDAN: No, no. I'm sorry. It's just... you remind me of someone.

EMILY: Who?

JORDAN: A friend of mine. We met in a class in college. She was a lot like you.

EMILY: An old flame?

JORDAN: No. It wasn't that kind of relationship. We were just good friends who had similar interests and passions.

EMILY: What passions?

JORDAN: We were both very concerned about the state of things.

EMILY: The state of things?

JORDAN: (*sighs*) Oh, it just seems that there's a rampant lack of respect and compassion in this world.

EMILY: Oh, don't I know it? People just seem to enjoy being rude to each other. They're so focused on themselves all the time.

JORDAN: And their money.

EMILY: Yeah, right. It's about getting and getting. They never have enough.

JORDAN: They take and take and take.

EMILY: When they get some, they just want more.

JORDAN: Pervasive lust and greed. And when they realize their lives are not the perfect dream, they turn to distractions, aversions, and addictions: alcohol, drugs, sex, you name it.

EMILY: It's like we have no center, no balance, no basic set of ideals.

JORDAN: (*sits up*) Exactly! We have lost our way.

EMILY: Oh, it's so true. It's like we have gone adrift in a sea of despair.

JORDAN: A poet with a big heart!

EMILY: But how do we get it back? How do we come back to balance?

JORDAN: We have to open our minds. We have to remove the blinders from our eyes and the plugs from our ears. We need to connect to the wisdom that is all around us. We can feel the awesome power that is beyond all of us.

EMILY: (*looks strangely at JORDAN*) Are you sure you're not one of those...

JORDAN: (*leans back*) Look! I'm not trying to push anything on you. I just thought we might connect with each other because you seemed like a nice person–someone who might share some of my same interests and curiosities about the world, that's all.

EMILY: Some people want to come up with this easy answer for the world's problems. You know, if we all just believed the right way, everything would be OK with the world.

JORDAN: But that's the problem right there, isn't it?

EMILY: What do you mean?

JORDAN: I mean that we like to think that all we have to do is believe the right thing but belief isn't enough. We need to engage with the world. We need to take action to make the changes we want to see.

EMILY: So you're an activist.

JORDAN: I believe I am... in the truest sense of the word. I believe in taking action. I believe in a greater power that can help us make the world better. I believe in the power of prayer.

EMILY: (*hesitates*) I... see.

JORDAN: No, wait. Just hear me out and then you can go on your way, if you like.

EMILY: (*Rises*) I could just go on my way now.

JORDAN: Wait! I can prove it.

EMILY: You can prove that prayer works?

JORDAN: Yes. (*beat*) Look! If you don't believe me then nothing's changed, right? I'm not keeping you here.

EMILY: You can PROVE that prayer works... beyond a doubt.

JORDAN: Yes.

EMILY: (*hesitates, then slowly sits*) OK. You've got my attention.

JORDAN: (*waits until EMILY sits*) It starts with a feeling.

EMILY: A feeling?

JORDAN: Tell me you've never felt it.

EMILY: Felt what?

JORDAN: That tingling at the back of your neck. That sensation that makes you take in a quick breath of surprise. That moment when you realize you are more than you thought you were.

EMILY: Sure, but what's that to do with prayer?

JORDAN: That's how it begins. There's a feeling, a connection, and then you understand and you get the message.

EMILY: The message?

JORDAN: That there's hope. (*beat*) Imagine it! You are feeling lonely, lost, unsure and then you suddenly know that things can be better, that the world can really be a place of peace.

EMILY: And that's where prayer comes in?

JORDAN: Yes. You open your mind. You open your heart and you ask for forgiveness. You ask for a better world.

EMILY: Just like that? You ask for it, you pray for it and it just happens?

JORDAN: Well, no.

EMILY: I thought you said that prayer works.

JORDAN: It does. I can prove it.

EMILY: You said that but I don't hear any proof.

JORDAN: I belong to a group.

EMILY: A group? What kind of group?

JORDAN: A group of believers...

EMILY: I see.

JORDAN: (*leans in*) We got a message. All of us–at the same time. It was undeniable.

EMILY: What sort of message?

JORDAN: (*dramatically*) The end of the world.

EMILY: (*pauses*) The end of the world?

JORDAN: The world has come to a tipping point. Surely you can see that. There's too much violence, drugs, war, gangs, dirty politicians, and all the rest. There had to come a time when it would all end.

EMILY: The end of the world.

JORDAN: Right. We knew it. It was being foretold to us. Humanity was given a final warning–to us.

EMILY: A warning?

JORDAN: We had come together for a prayer meeting when we received the message together–all at once.

EMILY: And what was the message?

JORDAN: That the whole world would be obliterated, annihilated in one day. Everything would be wiped out–everything. The slate would be wiped clean. The world would have to start over again.

EMILY: Well... I suppose nothing lasts forever. Even our own sun will one day burn out and the earth could be swallowed by a black hole but...

[SERVER enters with food and puts it on the table. S/he stops and stares when hearing about the end of the world.]

JORDAN: You don't understand. We were given a specific date.

EMILY: You were told exactly when the world would end?

JORDAN: Yes!

SERVER: Oh my! The world is going to end? No wonder you're in such a hurry.

EMILY: (*to SERVER*) Don't worry. It's just part of the play.

SERVER: Oh, right. The play. Is the wedding part of the end of the world?

JORDAN: It's complicated.

[EMILY and JORDAN stare at the SERVER until s/he leaves]

EMILY: (*to JORDAN*) OK. The end of the world is coming. Should I clear my calendar? When's the day?

JORDAN: October 6th.

EMILY: October 6th?

JORDAN: (*gets excited*) Yes!

EMILY: The entire world is going to end on October 6th?

JORDAN: Yes, yes!

EMILY: October 6th (*a beat*) was yesterday!

JORDAN: (*very excited*) Yes, that's right! The world was going to end yesterday! (*spreads arms and stands*) Everything...

everything you see here would have been gone. Every person you ever knew would have been vaporized in a maelstrom of heat and poisonous gas.

EMILY: (*shocked*) But... we're still here.

JORDAN: Yes! We are still here, still alive, still breathing.

EMILY: So... what happened?

JORDAN: (*sits*) That's the miracle. That's the proof. YOU are the proof. The fact that you are alive and breathing and here with me right now is the proof of the power of prayer.

EMILY: I don't understand.

JORDAN: We knew it was coming–the destruction of the world. We had been foretold and we knew we had to do something, anything we could do to save it. So, we prayed. We bowed our heads and opened our hearts and we begged to be saved. And... it worked. We have all been given another chance. Isn't it wonderful?

EMILY: And you and your people did this? You saved the world.

JORDAN: (*proudly*) Yes.

EMILY: All by yourselves?

JORDAN: Yes.

EMILY: Just by praying?

JORDAN: All through the night. (*a beat*) So, do you believe me now?

EMILY: I believe that YOU believe you!

JORDAN: Well, it's OK. You don't have to believe me. I know it's a lot to take in but I know what we did. The people of the world may never know how we saved them from destruction but WE know and WE can be proud of our work.

EMILY: (*starts to rise but then stops*) Well, I really should be… (*stops to think then sits back down*) There's just one thing I don't understand. (*a beat*) Are you here to date me or convert me?

JORDAN: Well, a little of both, I suppose. I saw your profile and I was intrigued. I hoped we might become friends, or more and, I have to admit, I hoped in the process you might become interested in what I do and want to join us.

EMILY: Fair enough but why come here? Why the dating app? Why not just pray your perfect partner into existence? I mean if prayer can save the world surely it can help manifest the love of your life.

JORDAN: Well, it doesn't really work like that.

EMILY: Oh, really?

JORDAN: Prayer is not for selfish needs or personal desires. There's a sacrifice that has to be part of it. You have to sacrifice time, or money, or even your own dignity, perhaps. You have to surrender to a higher wisdom, a higher power. If you can do that, change can be affected.

EMILY: (*leans forward slowly*) Oh, I didn't realize there was so much honor and commitment involved.

JORDAN: Well, yes. People don't really understand what is involved, the responsibility, the obligation.

EMILY: How noble!

JORDAN: Oh, now you're just playing with me. You want to make me think I might have a chance with you. (*EMILY is silent*) That maybe we could do this again sometime. (*EMILY just smiles*) That maybe we could do great things together.

[*EMILY places a hand over JORDAN's for a moment then stands and picks up the plate with her doughnut.*]

JORDAN: So? Shall we meet here again tomorrow for breakfast?

EMILY: No.

JORDAN: Another day, perhaps.

EMILY: Not a chance. Not even if the world is about to end.

[*EMILY reaches over, takes JORDAN's doughnut off his plate and puts it on hers then starts to leave.*]

JORDAN: Hey! That's my doughnut.

EMILY: Consider it your sacrifice. (*EMILY exits*)

Curtain

Pain In The Neck

A Ten-Minute Comedy

Cast

ERNEST - a Vampire dressed as a Vampire Hunter.

BRYANA - A Vampire Hunter dressed as a Vampire.

JANE - a party goer. She carries a small handbag.

Note: The parts can be played by persons of any gender or ethnicity. Pronouns may be changed as needed.

Scene

A costume party. There should be some music and the sounds of people at a party. At center stage are three chairs.

Time

Present.

[At rise, the stage is bare. After a moment, ERNEST enters and sits down looking tired. After another moment, BRYANA enters with a bag and sits near ERNEST.]

Script

ERNEST: Quite the party, huh?

BRYANA: (*sets down the bag*) I'll say. I love all the costumes, though.

ERNEST: Yeah. There are certainly some very creative people here.

BRYANA: (*looks at ERNEST*) If you don't mind me asking what are you supposed to be?

ERNEST: Oh, it's not obvious? I'm a Vampire Hunter.

BRYANA: A Vampire Hunter. Should I be worried? I mean, you CAN tell that I'm dressed as a vampire.

ERNEST: Oh, yes. You have an excellent costume but I wouldn't worry if I were you. You're not a real vampire.

BRYANA: How can you be so sure? I mean, I could be here looking for my next victim, looking for some fresh and delicious red blood.

[At the sound of the word "blood" ERNEST tries to hide himself as he licks his lips]

ERNEST: Blood? Oh, that's, uh, disgusting. Besides, you are too nice to be a real vampire. They are vicious and cruel and terrible at conversations.

BRYANA: I didn't know that.

ERNEST: And they hate beer. Blah! Not likely to find one at a party like this.

BRYANA: How do you know so much about vampires?

ERNEST: Oh, uh, I watch a lot of movies. I have a bit of an insomnia problem.

[There is the sound of phone music.]

BRYANA: Hang on. Just a minute. I just got a text. I want to make sure one of my friends isn't throwing up somewhere.

ERNEST: Of course! We wouldn't want that!

[BRYANA pulls out her cellphone, says a few words, and

then puts it away again.]

BRYANA: One of my friends is just having a cramp in her neck. She'll be all right.

ERNEST: (*with unusual interest*) Her neck?

BRYANA: Yeah. Right about here.

[BRYANA exposes part of her neck. ERNEST leans in cautiously to get a good look.]

ERNEST: Oooh! Maybe I could help.

BRYANA: (*quickly covers her neck*) Are you a doctor?

ERNEST: A kind of chiropractor. I do a lot of work on necks.

[BRYANA pulls her phone out again and hits a switch.]

BRYANA: I think I'm going to just turn this off for a while. They're very distracting wouldn't you agree?

ERNEST: What do you mean?

BRYANA: Cellphones. They're very distracting yet we can't seem to give them up.

ERNEST: Don't have one.

BRYANA: You don't have a cellphone? How do you stay in touch with people?

ERNEST: Oh, I flit about from place to place. I like to stay in close contact with my, uh, friends

BRYANA: You visit all your friends often?

ERNEST: It's almost an obsession with me.

[JANE enters and sits down in a chair next to ERNEST. As JANE talks, ERNEST stares at her neck and slowly starts to lean in.]

JANE: Phew! What a party. I don't think I know half these people and I thought I knew everyone. And now they all have costumes which, of course, makes it even more difficult to tell who's who. Have you seen these costumes? I mean some of them are really great. You can tell people really put some work into them. And are they scary! Did you see the zombies hanging around the punch bowl? They're really creepy. Makes you want to skip the punch and head right to the liquor cabinet. You know what I mean? (*notices ERNEST leaning toward her*) What are you doing?

ERNEST: (*looks directly into JANE's eyes*) Oh, my dear. You are fascinating!

JANE: (*slowly caught under ERNEST's spell*) I am?

ERNEST: Oh yes! You have a keen insight on the world.

JANE: I do?

[BRYANA begins to take notice.]

ERNEST: Oh yes. And you have a most exquisite neck!

JANE: I do?

ERNEST: Let me just give it a little friendly kiss.

JANE: A little? Friendly kiss? Well, I, uh.

ERNEST: Yes, just a little friendly...

[Just before ERNEST goes in for a bite, BRYANA pulls JANE up out of her seat.]

BRYANA: (*to JANE*) Hey! You know what would be really great right now? Another drink. That's what we all need. Another drink. How about it? You think you could go get us some more drinks while I have a nice little chat with our friend here? (*shakes JANE to break the spell*)

What do you say, huh? Drinks? Now?

JANE: (*turns attention to BRYANA*) What?

BRYANA: Drinks! Be a friend and get us another round of drinks.

JANE: (*dazed*) Drinks? Sure? Uh, what do you...

BRYANA: Anything wet.

[BRYANA pushes JANE offstage then turns to ERNEST.]

BRYANA: You're no Vampire Hunter!

ERNEST: And you're no Vampire.

BRYANA: It seems we both chose our alter egos for costumes.

ERNEST: It seems so. So what now? Are you going to pull out one of those nasty wooden fence posts you people carry around with you and run me through the heart with it?

BRYANA: That's old school. Nowadays we just fire a blast of ultraviolet light and then take you to one of our black site dentists to neuter you.

ERNEST: I think I'd rather have the stake.

BRYANA: We're trying to be more humane.

ERNEST: Then why not just let me go?

BRYANA: You know I can't do that.

ERNEST: So you are going to just capture me nicely?

BRYANA: That's the idea.

ERNEST: Well, that's very thoughtful of you. (*looks deeply into BRYANNA's eyes*) You are such a kind person. I would love to know more about you, to get closer to you...

[BRYANNA picks up her bag, pulls out a donut, and

flashes it at ERNEST.]

BRYANA: Your powers are useless on me, demon.

ERNEST: (*cowers in fear then notices the donut*) What is that?

BRYANA: It's a circle. A symbol that represents the essence of all religions. We're trying to be more inclusive.

ERNEST: It's a donut!

BRYANA: Well, I didn't have breakfast. (*takes a bite*)

ERNEST: Well, you're going to have to do better than that to take down a prince of the darkness. (*approaches BRYANA*)

[JANE enters carrying some drinks]

JANE: Here's your drinks. Got you some punch. Thank goodness those disgusting zombies moved on to the dance floor.

ERNEST: Aha! (*grabs JANE*)

JANE: Hey! You made me spill the drinks!

ERNEST: I have all I need to drink right here.

BRYANA: Don't do it, Vlad, or whatever your name is.

ERNEST: Actually, it's Ernest.

BRYANA: Ernest? You're kidding, right?

JANE: (*struggling*) Hey! Get your hands off of me!

[JANE reaches into her bag, pulls out some pepper spray, and sprays it at ERNEST who cries out and releases JANE.]

ERNEST: Ahhh! What was that?

JANE: Pepper spray, you creep!

ERNEST: But I am immune to such things!

BRYANA: Face it, Ernest! Your blood sucking days are over.

ERNEST Never! I have been here for thousands of years and I will be around for a thousand more.

[ERNEST begins frantically flapping his arms as if he could fly away.]

JANE: Is he a real vampire?

BRYANA: He thinks he is. (*notices ERNEST*) What are you doing?

ERNEST: I am trying to fly away but my bat powers are not working. I think that pooper spray has curtailed my strength.

JANE: It's pepper spray.

ERNEST: Whatever! I just need a little updraft here and I'll be off.

[ERNEST runs offstage still flapping his arms. There is a crashing sound offstage. ERNEST walks back onstage looking disheveled. He sits in the middle chair.]

ERNEST: I'm getting too old for this. You know, you get to a certain age where you know there's more millenia behind you than ahead of you.

BRYANA: Well, this is a first: a depressed Vampire.

JANE: Oh, you poor demented monster. Tell us all about your delusions!

ERNEST: You don't think I'm real, do you?

JANE: Well, of course not. There's no such thing as... are there?

BRYANA: Take a picture of him. That will settle the issue for certain.

JANE: Are you kidding?

BRYANNA: You have your phone with you?

JANE: Yeah.

BRYANNA: Go on. Take a picture.

JANE: Well, alright.

[JANE takes her cellphone out of her bag and snaps a picture of ERNEST then looks at the result.]

JANE: (*looking at her phone*) What? There's something wrong! He's not in the picture. Everything else is but he's not. Maybe there's something wrong with the camera.

BRYANNA: There's nothing wrong with your camera.

ERNEST: It's like mirrors. My image cannot be captured since I have no soul.

BRYANNA: So you ARE the real thing!

JANE: Well, that explains a lot. So, now what? A big old piece of wood jammed clean through his heart? Shoot him repeatedly with a silver bullet? Tie him down until the sun rises and his body burns and smolders?

BRYANA: (*looks at JANE with disgust*) We don't do that anymore.

JANE: What DO you do?

ERNEST: The same thing they do to cats.

BRYANA: (*sits next to ERNEST*) Oh, come on. It's not like that. We put you up in a rehabilitation center. They have some that are right off the ocean. You spend your days walking the beach, doing therapy, water aerobics, pickleball, you get a transfusion, some detox, maybe even some botox. Before you know it you'll be a new, uh, man.

ERNEST: Maybe you're right. I've been doing this since before your great grandparents thought you could get pregnant from heavy petting. It gets old. I'm getting old. My doctor says I am getting too much iron. My back is sore from all that flying and I can't see as well as I used to. I keep running into telephone poles and billboards. I've never seen a sunrise. Do you know how uncomfortable it can be to sleep in a coffin every night? Makes you claustrophobic. (*sighs*) Maybe it would be good to spend some time at the sea and get a new life.

JANE: But don't you want to live forever?

ERNEST: Oh, my dear. Immortality is not all it is cracked up to be. You spend all your time watching everyone else die. Just because I live forever doesn't mean I don't age. Every hundred years comes with yet another ache or pain. My arthritis is creeping through my body like frozen water pipes in the Winter. Besides, I'm bored beyond belief. I've seen every museum, every exhibit, every masterpiece. I've read every great book, seen every movie, watched every play ever written. Every new thing that comes out just seems like a repackaged version of all the old things. I've been to every natural wonder and human made wonder. I've seen and heard and smelled and tasted it all. There's nothing left to thrill me.

JANE: Being a Vampire really sucks, huh?

ERNEST: (*stares at JANE*) Never heard that one before! (*sighs*) Sometimes I actually envy you humans. You get a chance to experience all the wonders of the world and of each other. You get to share different and fascinating ideas with each other. You can participate in this constantly evolving and beautiful world filled with so many fascinating beings. All I do is sleep and chase necks all night. At my age it is getting harder and harder to catch them. It's exhausting. Maybe it's time for a change.

BRYANA: So? What do you say? You going to come back with me and take a little tour of Club Dead? I promise they serve garlic-free meals.

ERNEST: OK, sure. What harm can there be in looking just as long as we can get there before dawn?

BRYANA: Don't worry. They're open 24 hours.

ERNEST: Well, then. Let's go.

[BRYANA helps ERNEST walk offstage.]

JANE: (*looking offstage*) Hey! Wait for me. Does that place do anything for werewolves?

[JANE exits while howling like a wolf.]

<u>Curtain</u>

Property List:

- Paper bag
- Donut
- Something imitating pepper spray
- Small handbag for JANE

Perfect Partner

A Ten-Minute Comedy

Cast

STACI - (f) a middle aged self-assured person. She is moderately dressed.

CHASE - (m) a middle aged person in search of a date. He is dressed moderately nice.

BRANDI - (a) The bartender.

Note: The parts can be played by persons of any gender or ethnicity. Pronouns may be changed as needed.

Scene

A typical bar. There are sounds of people talking in the background. There might also be some music. The bar has napkins and silverware.

Time

Present.

Script

[At rise, STACI is seated at the bar with a drink. She is reading a book while nibbling on a snack. After a few moments, CHASE enters.]

CHASE: (*sees STACI and moves to the seat next to her*) This seat taken?

STACI: (*without looking up from her book*) Nope.

CHASE: You mind if I sit here?

STACI: It's a free country.

[*CHASE sits and waves his hand as if to order a drink. He looks around and then looks at STACI.*]

CHASE: So, you from around here?

STACI: (*puts down the book*) Look! You asked to sit there, so sit there. I would just like to read my book and drink my drink.

CHASE: (*a little startled*) Yeah, OK. No problem. (*thinks about leaving but changes his mind*) You know, I didn't mean anything by it. I just thought...

STACI: You just thought that the only reason a woman would sit alone at a bar is because she is lonely and is looking for some brave man to come save her. What makes you think...

[*CHASES's drink arrives.*]

STACI: (*takes a breath*) Oh, never mind. I'm sorry. Enjoy your drink. (*returns to her book*)

[*CHASE contemplates leaving again but then stirs his drink and thinks for a moment.*]

CHASE: You know, you're right. That IS what I was thinking and I never realized how unfair that really is. I mean, you have as much right as anyone else to just sit there in peace and enjoy your reading.

STACI: (*without looking up*) Thank you.

CHASE: (*thinks for a moment*) Why don't you let me make it up to you? Let me buy you another drink. (*waves for the bartender*)

STACI: (*sighs*) Don't want another drink.

CHASE: You sure? Looks like you have quite a ways yet to get through that book. I'd say there's at least a couple drinks left in that volume.

STACI: (*forcefully closes the book*) I'm married, OK?

CHASE: Yes, well, uh. OK. But, we're just having a conversation, right? (*a beat*) I, uh, couldn't help but notice that you're not wearing a ring.

STACI: You just happened to notice?

CHASE: Old habit.

STACI: Not everyone wears a ring. They are just symbols of possession and power. A band of cold metal cannot symbolize the warmth and comfort of real love. Rings are bands of ownership not companionship, of patrimony rather than matrimony.

CHASE: I guess when you look at it that way...

STACI: It comes from the days when women were taken and then tied up in ropes as property. They literally "tied the knot". The ropes were exchanged with rings but the meaning remains the same.

CHASE: I, uh, had no idea.

STACI: Of course not. You're a man.

CHASE: And yet you're married.

STACI: Happily married.

CHASE: And he shares these same thoughts about rings?

STACI: Why must it be a he? He could be a she.

CHASE: IS she a she and not a he or a them?

STACI: She is.

CHASE: I see (*thinks*)

STACI: You better order some ice water, pal.

CHASE: Huh?

STACI: Those thoughts in your head are going to fry a few circuits. Clean up your act!

CHASE: You have no idea what I am thinking.

STACI: I have a pretty good idea and it ain't going to happen.

CHASE: Oh come on. I am capable of having thoughts related to things other than sex. (*a beat*) At least tell me a little bit about her.

STACI: If I do, will you promise to go away?

CHASE: Cross my heart. (*crosses heart*)

STACI: Alright. (*changes posture*) She's about my age, about my height, she likes a lot of the things I like. We grew up in the same place.

CHASE: Sounds like a good match.

STACI: It's a perfect match.

CHASE: Like two peas in a pod?

STACI: Like the same pea in the pod.

CHASE: What? Did you marry your twin sister or something?

STACI: I married myself.

CHASE: You did what? Wait, can you even do that?

STACI: It's not a legal commitment but I didn't do it for legal recognition.

CHASE: Then why did you do it?

STACI: It was an act of affirmation. I don't need a man or a woman, a puppy, or a hydrangea to complete me. I don't need to find a better half when I know I am already whole.

CHASE: OK, but why get married? Why the dog and pony show if you just want to be on your own?

STACI: Because I wanted to be a bride. I've looked forward to the pageantry and opulence of a big wedding since I was a little girl. Just because I don't want to be shackled with the frailties and shortcomings of another human being doesn't mean I don't want to have the grand ceremony promised to me.

CHASE: So you did the whole thing: the organ, the dress, the vows, the preacher?

STACI: The whole thing.

CHASE: How did you do the part with the kiss?

STACI: We skipped that part.

CHASE: And the first dance at the reception?

STACI: Turns out the preacher was a pretty good dancer.

CHASE: Hmm. (*rolls his drink in his hands then takes a big gulp to finish it*)

STACI: You can buy me that drink now.

CHASE: (*waves down the BARTENDER and displays a "two" with his fingers*) I could use another one myself. (*a beat*) I guess I still don't get it. Why go through all that trouble just to make a statement to the world? Wouldn't it just be easier to say affirmations to yourself in the mirror?

STACI: I was in a really bad relationship. I felt trapped. I had been taught to just take it. Roll with the punches. Finally, I had enough. The thought of having children with that man was terrifying. When I finally got out I was a hot mess. My life was in shambles. What I needed was a confirmation of myself–of who I am and what I could be. I decided to marry the one person I knew I could trust and depend on. But, more than that, I wanted the world to see that I was strong, that I needed no one to be fully myself.

[*BARTENDER gives them their drinks*]

CHASE: Well, I guess if you put it that way.

STACI: Oh, now. Wait a minute! Don't tell me you actually understand.

CHASE: Well, I a dmit I don't get it completely but...

STACI: Oh please!

CHASE: Are you trying to tell me that just because I'm a man I can't understand the need to be seen and heard? I can't relate to self definition? I don't have times when I need confirmation?

STACI: Let's just say that I'm a little skeptical.

CHASE: Now who's being sexist?

STACI: Oh really? When you came prancing over here dripping with overconfidence were you thinking about the philosophical implications of the use of social media with adolescents or were you thinking about how to get into my pants?

CHASE: I was thinking how beautiful AND confident AND

intelligent you looked sitting there. I was thinking I wanted to come to know you.

STACI: Please! Save it for the bimbos looking for Mr. Money Bags.

CHASE: OK, you got me. I'm just another mindless male looking to continue the species.

STACI: Ever heard of the population explosion?

CHASE: Cut me a little slack here. I've been through my own rough times with partners I thought were as dedicated to the relationship as I was when all they were looking for was their own personal cheerleader and butler and daddy all rolled into one person. When I saw you sitting there alone I thought I might change my luck.

STACI: You might have better luck looking for a four leaf clover.

[*STACI returns to her book. CHASE plays with his drink and thinks. He glances over in STACI's direction.*]

CHASE: The... Girl... on... the... uh...

STACI: What?

CHASE: Your book. You're reading The Girl On The... Something.

STACI: The Girl On The Train.

CHASE: Paula Hawkins?

[*STACI puts the book down and turns slightly*]

STACI: (*surprised*) You know this book?

CHASE: It's been a few years.

STACI: (*suspicious*) So, what did you think of it?

CHASE: Well, I can see why you would be interested in it. The protagonist is struggling to get over her ex while she battles with her self-image and alcohol.

STACI: Huh! I would not have taken you for a reader.

CHASE: Not all men are neanderthals with big sticks.

STACI: The jury is still out. (*a beat*) Tell me more.

CHASE: The book? (*STACI nods*) Well, it seems to fixate on the unintended consequences of infidelity. Its characters are constantly mired in deceit and disappointment.

STACI: Interesting. A hint of insight. And what did you glean from the work?

CHASE: Maybe self marriage is the way to go.

STACI: Now you're just mocking me. (*picks up her book*)

CHASE: Ever considered it?

STACI: Considered what?

CHASE: Infidelity?

STACI: An affair... from myself?

CHASE: Well, at least you wouldn't have to worry about keeping it a secret.

STACI: It didn't take long to bring the conversation back to sex, did it?

CHASE: Wouldn't it be a little exciting? Maybe dangerous?

STACI: Because I might find out about me?

CHASE: Since you're already married you wouldn't have to suffer the pain of cheating or worry about ulterior motives.

STACI: Except my own.

CHASE: You seem like a very forgiving person.

STACI: Forget it! I don't have affairs.

CHASE: How noble of you, I...

STACI: With single men.

CHASE: What?

STACI: Strict rule. No affairs with single men.

CHASE: Oh, really? (*a beat*) Well, we can fix that.

STACI: Huh?

[*CHASE stands up to face the audience as if they are people in the bar. He holds up his glass and taps it with a spoon or something similar.*]

CHASE: Excuse me! May I have your attention please? (*waits for bar sounds to diminish*) I would like to invite all of you here to witness a matrimony between me and myself. Barkeep!

[*BRANDI enters. STACI looks shocked but then eventually starts to giggle.*]

CHASE: Barkeep, please ask me to repeat the following words...

BRANDI: Huh? I don't understand and you're causing a...

CHASE: Please! This is a very solemn occasion. It's not often that a man gets to marry someone with such high character and dignified reputation.

BRANDI: (*to STACI*) Her?

CHASE: Oh, no. She's already taken. The good ones always go first, you know. No, I am hitching up with the only other human being besides her that is worth devoting my life to–me!

BRANDI: But you can't...

CHASE: I can and I will so let's get on with it. (*raises hands and looks toward audience*) All these people are waiting for this special moment so they can get back to their watered down drinks and overly greasy food. It's a special day! Now, say "repeat after me."

BRANDI: OK.

CHASE: No. You say it… (*rolls his hands to encourage BRANDI*)

BRANDI: Oh, OK. Repeat after me.

CHASE: Do you, handsome guy at the bar…

BRANDI: Do you, handsome guy at the bar…

CHASE: Take this rather intelligent and dignified human specimen…

BRANDI: Take this, uh, guy?

CHASE: (*aside to BARTENDER*) Close enough. (*continues*) To be your less than lawfully wedded partner through sickness, health, drought, body odor, poor choices in food and fashion, and all the rest?

BRANDI: To be your…

CHASE: I do! And I pronounce me man and proudly blushing husband. (*walks toward audience*) Let's hear it folks! (*encourages the audience to clap then turns to STACI*) You may now kiss the husband.

[*STACI stares at CHASE for a moment and laughs. She then rises, moves toward CHASE, and gives him a long kiss.*]

STACI: What do you say we sneak away from this place?

CHASE: Are you suggesting we run away and have an affair?

STACI: I believe I am.

CHASE: Well, I won't say anything if you won't.

[*CHASE and STACI exit together*]

Curtain

Property List:

- Table or bar top
- Two chairs
- Drinks
- Napkins and utensils

Tooth Fairy

A Ten-Minute Comedy

Cast

ROGER - a single father.

TF - The Tooth Fairy dressed in a typical fairy outfit with wings, a wand, and a small bag.

ELISE - Roger's daughter.

Note: The parts can be played by persons of any gender or ethnicity. Pronouns may be changed as needed.

Scene

A bedroom.

Time

Present.

Script

[At rise, ELISE is tucked away under the covers of a bed. ROGER sits on or near the bed and looks at ELISE.]

ELISE: Daddy?

ROGER: Yes, sweetheart.

ELISE: Have you still got it?

ROGER: Got what?

ELISE: C'mon, daddy! Stop kidding.

ROGER: Well, let me see.

[ROGER pats his hand around his pockets as if looking for something.]

ROGER: Oh no! I can't seem to find it.

ELISE: Daddy!

ROGER: (*stops at his shirt pocket*) Wait a minute. (*reaches into the pocket and pulls out a small envelope*) Here it is!

ELISE: Can I see it again?

[ROGER opens the envelope and lets ELISE look inside.]

ROGER: There it is - one golden tooth.

ELISE: Daddy! It's not golden. It's just a normal tooth.

ROGER: Did it hurt coming out?

ELISE: Nope. Just popped out!

[ROGER closes the envelope and puts it back into his pocket]

ROGER: All safe and sound.

ELISE: But aren't you going to put it under my pillow?

ROGER: Why would I do a thing like that? Don't you remember the story of the princess and the pea? If I put it under your pillow you might not get a single wink of sleep.

ELISE: But if you don't put it under my pillow the Tooth Fairy won't come in the night and leave me money for it.

ROGER: You mean this little tooth is worth some money? Maybe

I should save it to help pay for a new car. Got anymore teeth in there?

ELISE: Daddy! Only the Tooth Fairy can turn a tooth into money and it's only for me.

ROGER: So you've cornered the market on the tooth exchange, have you?

ELISE: C'mon, Daddy! Put my tooth under my pillow so I can get some sleep.

ROGER: Well, I guess I'm not getting anything out of this deal. (*puts the envelope under ELISE's pillow*) There you go. Is my princess going to be able to sleep?

ELISE: I am perfectly fine.

ROGER: Good. Now you get some sleep so that you can wake up to your small fortune in the morning.

[ROGER tucks in ELISE and gets up to leave the room]

ELISE: Daddy?

ROGER: Yea, sweetie?

ELISE: Do you still miss mommy?

ROGER: (*goes back to ELISE*) Of course I do. Every day.

ELISE: Me too.

ROGER: Do you remember what I told you?

ELISE: That she will always live on in here. (*points to her heart*)

ROGER: That's right. She lives right here. (*points to his heart*) Now get some sleep.

ELISE: Will you stay with me just for a little while until I can get to sleep?

ROGER: What about the Tooth Fairy?

ELISE: Oh, she's got all night. She'll wait for you.

ROGER: OK. (*kisses ELISE*)

[ROGER leans back and gradually falls asleep. After a few moments, the Tooth Fairy arrives. She spreads a magic powder throughout the room. She walks over to ELISE and looks at her.]

TF: (*to ELISE*) There you are, my dear, fast asleep. (*looks at ROGER*) And who is this fine specimen of a human being next to you? (*starts to reach out to ROGER but stops herself*) We can look but we can't touch. (*turns to ELISE*) Let's see what you have for me, my young friend.

[TF reaches under ELISE's pillow. ELISE makes some sounds which makes TF cautious. Eventually she pulls out the envelope and retrieves the tooth. She waves her wand over the envelope, checks it, and then returns the envelope under the pillow. She puts the tooth in a container then puts it into her bag.]

TF: There you go! I'd stay and chat but I have a busy schedule to keep. (*looks at ROGER and sighs*) Maybe I will see you again. (*she gets up to leave but stops herself*) Maybe I could… I mean just one little one. What could it hurt? (*pause*) But it's against the rules. (*pause*) How could it possibly hurt? (*pause*) Rules, rules, rules! (*pause*) Oh, well. Sometimes you have to live on the edge!

[TF kisses ROGER on the cheek and then gets ready to leave. She hears ROGER start to wake and freezes.]

ROGER: Wha, what's going on here? (*sees TF*) Who are you? (*TF doesn't move*) Well? What are you doing in my house?

TF: You can see me?

ROGER: Of course I can see you. You look like a tree ornament or something from a bad cartoon.

[TF turns to ROGER, reaches into her bag, and desperately throws magic dust at him several times. ROGER wipes himself off.]

ROGER: What are you doing?

TF: It's my magic dust. It is supposed to keep people asleep so I can do my work.

ROGER: Work? What work? Are you some kind of badly dressed cat burglar?

[TF takes her wand and raps ROGER on the head with it.]

ROGER: Ow! What are you doing? You're a terrible thief.

TF: (*stares at the wand*) I don't understand. You're not supposed to be awake. The magic dust? The magic wand? Nothing is working. What could have happened? Am I losing my powers?

ROGER: You are clearly losing your mind!

TF: (*gasps*) Of course! The kiss! A kiss breaks all spells. (*to ROGER*) The moment I kissed you all the magical energy dissipated. Poof! Like a dust cloud in the desert.

ROGER: Wait! You kissed me?

TF: I know it's against protocol but it was just an innocent little kiss.

ROGER: What kind of strange burglar are you and how did you get in here?

TF: Why I flew of course. How do you expect me to visit so many children?

ROGER: You rob little children?

TF: Of course not, silly. I bring them gifts.

ROGER: Hold on! You're the… oh no, that's ridiculous.

[TF reaches into her bag, pulls out the container with the tooth and shows it to ROGER. ROGER stares at the tooth, looks at ELISE, and then looks at TF.]

ROGER: You! You're the Tooth Fairy?

TF: That's me! (*puts tooth away*)

ROGER: But you're not real!

TF: Oh yeah? (*pinches ROGER's cheek*) Believe me now?

ROGER: But I'm the one who leaves some money under her pillow. You're just some story we tell our children.

TF: Exactly! You get to believe what you want and she gets to believe what she wants.

ROGER: Then it's all just a big lie?

TF: It's part of learning to find hope. It's about seeking the best possibilities. You can't have hope without imagination and you can't have integrity if you don't think such a thing is possible.

ROGER: That's all just part of the set up for our fall into disillusionment.

TF: Oh my! You sound like someone who has suffered.

ROGER: (*softly*) Yes.

TF: And I am here to tell you that you should believe!

ROGER: Believe in what?

TF: The future! The Land of What-Ifs! The love of those still with you! (*glances at ELISE*) Believe in magic!

ROGER: Oh, I don't know. How can there be magic when love ends?

TF: But love never ends. It changes form, it may ebb and flow like a mighty ocean, it may be as soft as a whisper or as loud as a roar, but it is always there.

ROGER: (*stares at TF*) You are an amazing person.

TF: (blushing) Well, I'm a fairy, but...

ROGER: Maybe it's right here.

TF: What's here?

ROGER: The love you speak about.

TF: Well, of course it is! It's all around us. It's in the air and in the trees and in the sunshine and blowing in the breeze. It's... (*notices ROGER staring at her*)

ROGER: No. I mean what if it's right here!

TF: Oh, you mean right HERE here?

ROGER: Sometimes love is right in front of you and you just don't see it. Wouldn't you agree?

TF: Uh, well. Yes. I suppose so but...

ROGER: But, what? If magic happens, shouldn't we embrace it?

TF: But... I can't!

ROGER: You can't love?

TF: Of course I can but I can't... not with you.

ROGER: Why not?

TF: *(looks around)* It's against the rules.

ROGER: What would happen to you?

TF: I would lose my wings and my wand. I would become...

ROGER: A mere mortal?

TF: Yes.

ROGER: (*moves in to hold TF)* But then we could be together.

TF: Oh, no. I wouldn't know how to be a human.

ROGER: I think you know better than most. You are kind and loving. You are great with kids. You know more about kindness than most.

TF: Oh, Only know about love and dreams.

ROGER: Tell me, really. What more do we need to know than that? But, forgive me. I was being selfish. If you don't keep hope alive for all those young children and their little teeth, who else will?

TF: Oh, but I'm not the only one.

ROGER: You're not? I always thought it was a solo gig. You know, like Santa Claus and the Easter Bunny.

TF: Oh, well. Those two only have to work one day out of the year. Us tooth fairies are on the job all year long all across the world. We've got a small army of tooth traders out there.

ROGER: So maybe they won't miss one?

TF: Oh! I don't know. It's never been done before. (starts to pace) This is very unusual. I just don't know. How did I get in this mess?

ROGER: You kissed me.

TF: Oh yes. That's right. I guess it is partly my fault. (*walks up to ROGER*) Maybe I should kiss you again and see what happens. (*they kiss*) OH, my. That is magic.

ROGER: (*waits*) Well?

TF: (*still thinking*) Well, what?

ROGER: You and me? (*looks at ELISE*) You could help me bring up this beautiful young lady. We could help spread your words of love and compassion… together.

TF: Oh, that does sound lovely but… I can't.

ROGER: I don't understand.

TF: Don't you see? It would set a bad precedent. What if all the fairies decide to quit and settle down? Who would fill all those children with hope and wonder? Who would collect the teeth? Who would listen to the wishes we whisper in the wind? Who would hide colored eggs in the grass? Who would help fill all the presents at Christmas?

ROGER: I thought those were elves.

TF: Elves with wings. You don't think they take the bus to the north pole do you?

ROGER: I never thought about it.

TF: It could lead to the end of magic?

ROGER: But it might lead to the beginning of love!

TF: Oh, you are indeed a fine human and I would be lucky to spend my mortal days with you but it just can't be done.

ROGER: Afraid you might actually love being a mere human?

TF: Oh you silly mortal! You can't have hope if there is nothing to hope for. It is my job to whisper the possibilities into your ear. That is what I love. That is what I am meant to do. As wonderful as it might be to stay here with you I could never be happy because I would not fulfill my purpose.

ROGER: I understand.

TF: *(hugs ROGER)* OH you are a good man and your daughter is lucky to have you. I will come visit when I can and I will whisper in your ear when you stand in the breeze and I will smile at you when the rainbow appears. (she pulls away) I must go. There are always more teeth to collect.

ROGER: Goodbye! I won't forget you.

[TF exits with a typical fairy flourish. ROGER looks in her direction then hears ELISE stirring. He goes to ELISE.]

ELISE: Daddy?

ROGER: Yes?

ELISE: I just had this really weird dream. The Tooth Fairy came to take my tooth but then she was talking to somebody.

ROGER: Maybe she came to get your tooth. Let's see... (reaches under the pillow and grabs the envelope then opens it) Look here! A small fortune!

ELISE: Oh daddy, It's only a dollar.

ROGER: All great empires began with a dollar and a dream. Now get yourself back to sleep so you can start having some lucky dreams.

ELISE: How will I know which dreams are lucky?

ROGER: Oh, that's easy. Just listen to the whispers in the wind. Now you get some sleep. Good night!

ELISE: Good night, daddy! *(ROGER starts to leave but she stops him)* Daddy!

ROGER: Yea?

ELISE: I think I have another loose tooth.

ROGER: (*smiles*) That's good fortune indeed! Goodnight sweetheart!

<u>Curtain</u>

Property List:

- A small envelope
- Wand
- bag

Too Much Sheet

A Ten-Minute Drama

Cast

DALTON - An African-American fabric store clerk.

BRANDON - A white customer.

Note 1: The genders and racial background of these characters are important to the story. Any changes should reflect the main idea of the play.

Note 2: This play is based upon and is dedicated to the work of Darryl Davis.

Scene

The sales counter of a fabric store. There should be various pieces of fabric strewn about on a counter. There may also be other sewing items.

Time

Present.

Script

[At rise, DALTON is tending the sales counter. Some customers may precede BRANDON for effect. BRANDON the enters holding a folded sheet and pillowcase and

approaches the sales counter.]

DALTON: May I help you?

BRANDON: I, uh, would like to buy a sheet.

DALTON: a bedsheet?

BRANDON: Yeah.

DALTON: What size?

BRANDON: Huh?

DALTON: What size sheet do you want: twin, full, queen, king?

BRANDON: Uh, I don't know. One person size.

DALTON: OK, twin. What about the color?

BRANDON: White. And a white pillowcase.

[*BRANDON gets the sheet and pillowcase on puts them on the counter.*]

DALTON: One white sheet and one white pillowcase.

[*DALTON rings up the items while trying not to stare at BRANDON*]

DALTON: Anything else?

BRANDON: I need some scissors.

DALTON: What kind of scissors do you need?

BRANDON: There's different kinds?

DALTON: Sure. There's embroidery scissors, fabric shears, pinking shears, buttonhole, upholstery, papercraft, ceremonial scissors. There are even special snips for little kids for their arts and crafts projects. What kind do you need?

BRANDON: I just need some regular scissors.

DALTON: Well, what are you planning to cut?

BRANDON: The sheets.

DALTON: The sheets? (*picks up the sheets*) These sheets?

BRANDON: Yeah. I'm, uh, making a costume.

DALTON: Oh, I see. Going to a costume party?

BRANDON: Can I just get those scissors?

DALTON: Do you have a pattern?

BRANDON: A what?

DALTON: A pattern. It shows where to cut the holes for your costume. You're also going to need some needles and thread and maybe a marking pen and...

BRANDON: I don't need any of that stuff. I just need the scissors. Could you please just give me a normal pair of scissors?

DALTON: Scissors... Sure. (*takes out a pair of scissors and puts it on the counter*) Is that it?

BRANDON: Yeah. That's it. How much?

DALTON: You sure? You don't need some poster board?

BRANDON: Poster board. I ain't making no signs.

DALTON: For the hood.

BRANDON: Oh, yeah. For the...

[*BRANDON freezes as he realizes that DALTON might know what he's doing. DALTON just stares at him for a moment.*]

DALTON: You're going to need something to shape it with.

BRANDON: Uh...

DALTON: It's a rather distinctive shape, wouldn't you say?

BRANDON: Yeah. I'll take that too.

DALTON: That's some costume party you are going to.

[DALTON rings up the items and sets them on the counter to wait for payment. BRANDON reaches into his wallet to retrieve a credit card, looks at it, changes his mind, and starts to put it away.]

BRANDON: Um, you know, Just forget it. (*turns around to walk away*)

DALTON: (*calls out*) Can I just ask you one question? [*BRANDON stops*] You know you're going to have to go all the way across town to get to another fabric store? [*BRANDON doesn't move*] Look! I'm not going to say anything to anyone. You have every right to gather with whoever you want. No one's going to know it's you, anyways. Isn't that the whole point of the, uh, costume?

BRANDON: (*turns back*) Yeah. I guess it is. But, my name is on the card.

DALTON: No cash?

BRANDON: Nah.

DALTON: I tell you what. You take it and come back tomorrow with the money for it.
(*bags all the items*)

BRANDON: Why would you do that? I mean, you know what this is all about. Why would you help me?

[BRANDON reaches for the bag but DALTON does not let

it go]

DALTON: I just need you to answer me one question.

BRANDON: (*hesitantly*) What?

DALTON: Why?

BRANDON: Why what?

DALTON: Why do you hate me?

BRANDON: What are you talking about?

DALTON: You know what I'm talking about. You know nothing about me yet you hate me. Why?

BRANDON: I, uh, well, I don't hate YOU particularly.

DALTON: Just people who look like me?

BRANDON: You can't help it. It's just the way you are, the way you was made.

DALTON: The way I was made? What do you mean? Help me understand.

BRANDON: You can't understand.

DALTON: Try me.

BRANDON: Just look at our jails, the streets, the crime rate, what do you see?

DALTON: I see people who have been ignored and forgotten by the system. Jails and streets are filled with people who are constantly denied any opportunity to get ahead.

BRANDON: But you're different from us. It's obvious.

DALTON: I was born by my mother. You?

BRANDON: Well, yeah but...

DALTON: I grew up with my family and went to school and in the winters I sled down snowy hills and in the summers I ate ice cream. You?

BRANDON: Well, yeah, but...

DALTON: And when I grew up I drove my car too fast and I made out in the back seat and tried beer and cursed at the acne on my face. You?

BRANDON: Well, yeah, but...

DALTON: But, what? What makes me so different from you? What inflames a deep seated hatred for someone you know absolutely nothing about?

BRANDON: Well, because I know for a fact that you people have these genes.

DALTON: Genes? I assume you mean something we were born with not something we wear.

BRANDON: Yeah. You are all born with this violence gene.

DALTON: Violence gene? You mean I was born with a preponderance for hurting people? That I just can't help myself?

BRANDON: Well, yeah. It's been proven through history.

DALTON: (*leans in*) Then why am I not jumping over this counter right now and beating you into the floor?

BRANDON: (*hesitates*) I don't know.

DALTON: (*relaxes*) Because I have never hurt anyone in my life and you're not worth my changing that now. (*moves back*)

BRANDON: It's just that your gene has not come out yet.

DALTON: What?

BRANDON: It ain't switched on yet. I lies in waiting in some people until it gets turned on and then you get violent.

DALTON: Oh, is that how it works?

BRANDON: Yeah. It's science. Can't argue with that.

DALTON: Right. You can't argue with science. But if that's true then maybe I should be afraid of you?

BRANDON: Afraid of me? Why?

DALTON: Because you're a serial killer.

BRANDON: A what?

DALTON: Serial killer. You know, someone who deliberately kills and mutilates many people over an extended period of time.

BRANDON: But I ain't no...

DALTON: Maybe not yet but it's in your genes.

BRANDON: What?

DALTON: Ever heard of Jack the Ripper? Ted Bundy? Jeffrey Dahmer?

BRANDON: Well yeah, but, I ain't like any of them.

DALTON: John Wayne Gacy? The Zodiac Killer? David Berkowitz?

BRANDON: I told you I ain't like any of those people.

DALTON: Richard Ramirez, the Night Stalker, ever heard of him? He killed and tortured dozens of people. How about Albert DeSalvo, the supposed Boston Strangler who liked to choke elderly women, heard of him? Or, maybe you're familiar with Robert Alcala, the serial killer who showed up on an episode of The Dating Game while he was brutally choking hundreds of women. Know him?

BRANDON: (*frustrated*) I ain't no serial killer I told you.

DALTON: Did you know all those men were white? An overwhelming majority of serial killers are solitary white men... like you. White men must have a serial killer gene in them. (*a beat*) It's been proven through history.

BRANDON: That's ridiculous. Just because a man is born white doesn't mean he's a...

DALTON: He's what? A brutal violent killer?

BRANDON: That don't make any sense.

DALTON: Can't argue with science!

BRANDON: (*quietly*) Yeah. (*a beat*) But that ain't the worst of it.

DALTON: Do tell.

BRANDON: You people are taking our jobs.

DALTON: (*sighs*) And what do you do?

BRANDON: I fix up cars. I'm good at it too.

DALTON: And clearly it's prepared you for work in the clothing industry.

BRANDON: Huh?

DALTON: How long have you been fixing cars?

BRANDON: I don't know. Since I was a kid.

DALTON: And you're still doing it?

BRANDON: Yeah, so?

DALTON: You're STILL doing the same job you've always done.

BRANDON: That's right. What of it?

DALTON: So no one has taken your job away yet?

BRANDON: Oh yeah, what about you? Whose job did you take?

DALTON: You assume that I have taken over someone else's job.

BRANDON: Well, yeah.

DALTON: What if I told you I was the manager of this store?

BRANDON: The manager? You ain't no manager.

DALTON: (*looks serious then laughs*) OK. You got me. I'm not the manager.

BRANDON: I knew it. You couldn't possibly be a...

DALTON: (*serious*) I'm the owner.

BRANDON: The owner?

DALTON: Yeah, the owner. I worked hard and long to make the money I needed to buy this place. After a whole lot of toil and sweat I made enough and I bought the store. Now it's mine and you're here, in MY store, buying your... outfit.

[*DALTON pushes the shopping bag towards BRANDON but BRANDON does not take it. BRANDON stares at the bag for a moment.*]

BRANDON: You can keep it. (*pushes the package back*)

Curtain

Property List:

- White sheet, folded
- White pillowcase, folded
- Scissors

- Sheet of poster board or cardboard
- Shopping bag

Other Books

Spirituality

Many Leaves, One Tree: A Collection of Aphorisms Inspired By The Tao Te Ching

The Purpose Derived Life: What In The Universe Am I Here For?

Three Guidelines For Ethical Living

Prayers

The Emergence of God: The Intersection of Science, Nature, and Spirituality

Emergent Spirituality: Principles and Practices at the Intersection of Science, Nature, and Spirituality

Open Hearts and Open Doors: Radical Hospitality

Let Us Wander: A Ministry of Music and Arts

Games

52 New Card Games (For Those Old Cards)

36 New Dice Games

40 Games For Forty Dice

The Langer Deck (an oracle deck)

Playing Cards and the Game of Living Well

Castle Imbroglio: An Escape Adventure Book

Music

A Guide to the Art of Musical Performance

A Theory For All Musics

- Book 1: Fundamentals
- Book 2: Chords and Part Writing
- Book 3: The Tools of Parametric Analysis
- Book 4: Parametric Analysis

Rounds and Canons For Peace and Justice

Songs of Worship

50 Songs For Meditation

Fiction

The Milleran Cluster Series

- Book 1: Of Eternal Light
- Book 2: The Forever Horizon
- Book 3: The Song of the Mother
- Book 4: The Song of the Mother
- The Journey of Awri

Theater

Four Comedies

10 x 10 - Ten Ten-Minute Plays, Book 1

10 x 10 - Ten Ten-Minute Plays, Book 2

10 x 10 - Ten Ten-Minute Plays, Book 3

10 x 10 - Ten Ten-Minute Plays, Book 4

Ageless Wisdom: Multigenerational Plays For Worship

Poetry

Looking At The World: A Collection of Original Poetry

Final Note

If you enjoyed reading this book please let me know and please consider writing a positive online review.

Thank you!

Kenneth P. Langer

About The Author

Kenneth P. Langer

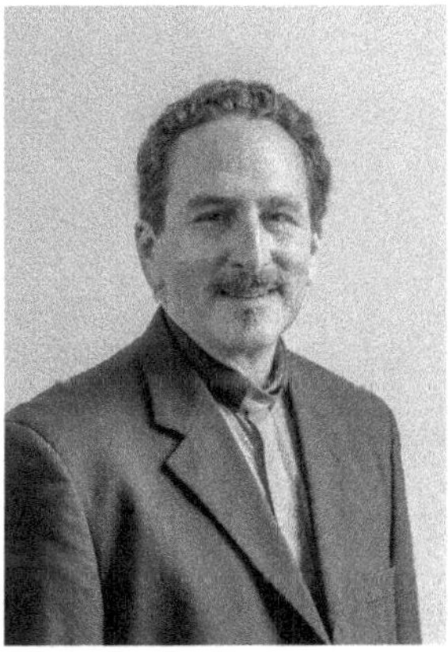

Kenneth P. Langer is an ordained Universalist minister and a former college professor with graduate degrees in both music and theology. He is a published writer, composer, and poet and is the author of several works of fiction as well as books on spiritual living. He also enjoys playing and designing games.

Learn more by visiting his website:
http://kennethplanger.com

He can be contacted at:
klangerdude@gmail.com

Contact Information

personal web site:

https://sites.google.com/site/klangerdude/

book site:

http://brassbellbooks.com

email:
klangerdude@gmail.com

www.ingramcontent.com/pod-product-compliance
Lightning Source LLC
LaVergne TN
LVHW010104110826
845155LV00028B/478
* 9 7 8 1 9 4 9 4 6 4 3 0 6 *